Branko Bokun

BIOECONOMY
MATRIARCHY IN POST-CAPITALISM

Vita Books
42 Wandsworth Bridge Road
London SW6 2TH

First published 1994
by Vita Books
42 Wandsworth Bridge Road
London SW6 2TH

ISBN 0 9510525 5 1

1. Economics   2. Politics   3. Sociology   4. Title

Printed and bound in Great Britain by
Biddles Ltd, Guildford and King's Lynn

My thanks to Anne Loudon for her help in writing this book.

My thanks also to Flavia Campilli and Misha Lukic for their assistance.

CONTENTS

INTRODUCTION

Our economic life has been mainly guided by abstract theories or wishful speculations which has brought our life and the life on our planet to danger. Economics is not a positive science. Economics is a creation of the mind, its beliefs and its ideologies. In fact, each ideology has its own economics.

In order to see what kind of economics would be in our best interest and in the interest of our planet in the long run, we must unearth what our real nature is, the true meaning of life.

In essence, life consists of activities caused by biochemical instability, which we know as discomfort or irritation, a state of fear. Life is inorganic matter in a highly unstable state of existence created by the particularly mild atmospheric conditions on our planet. These special conditions increase the instability of the atoms and molecules of certain extra sensitive elements, forcing them into activity in search of a lesser instability. Life is forced on matter by the conditions on our planet.

Basically, life consists of the biochemical discomfort's need to find a lesser discomfort.

This need creates receptors and receptivity, which generate perceptors and perceptivity which in turn create senses and sensitivity.for whatever can reduce or placate biochemical discomfort.

The main aim of life and its activity is to achieve a lesser instability, lesser fear. Everything that exists has been forced into existence by the instability imposed by external forces. Every existence gravitates towards its previous state of existence.

This biochemical instability provides vital energy helping the instability towards a lesser instability, lesser discomfort, lesser irritation, lesser fear.

Living matter tries to reduce its instability or precariousness, its frustrations or fears, by expanding. Any growth in nature is caused by an irritation or a frustration. Without being irritated the amino acids would never become

1

proteins, without being irritated nucleic acids would never become genes, without being irritated a cell would never become two cells, without being irritated cells would never have created multicellular organisms. If the central nervous system of our ancestors had not been highly irritated we would have never developed our big brain.

The main paradox of life is that growth, while trying to reduce instability or irritation, creates complexity, thereby increasing vulnerability and precariousness. Complexity increases vulnerability and precariousness because it increases needs. In fact, life generates its own end, its death. Striving to reduce instability or irritation through growth or expansion, living organisms over-grow. It is in the nature of an over-growth to end in a breakdown or death. The life of an organism reaches its end through over-expansion. It is over-expansion which leads to explosion, to decay.

In order to understand the evolution of our species and our speculative wishful reasoning better, it might help to analyse how species evolves from another species. In order to understand our past we must abandon the conceit of thinking that we are the supreme achievement of evolution. Our ecological crisis, which is created by man and which is endangering life on our planet, should start us doubting about conceit.

In order to be able to put things right, we must begin by discovering where or when we went wrong.

A new species could only evolve through the more vulnerable and unstable individuals of the previous species. Successful individuals of a species tend to perpetuate the same species. Certain insects and reptiles for example have hardly changed since their appearance.

The more unstable or the more vulnerable individuals of a species tend to be driven from the group, or to escape from the environment dominated by the more successful and better equipped. Many of these more vulnerable individuals perish in the new environment, but those who survive start a new species.

Frustration, irritation and the needs of the escapees in the new habitat force an increase in the growth of their nervous systems, of their brains and the brains' activities.

Escaping from the better equipped procariotic cells,

the more vulnerable of these cells, thus more open to changes, opened the way to the formation of more complex eucariotic cells. The ancestors of reptiles must have escaped from their better equipped cousins of the sea. The ancestors of mammals must have escaped from their better equipped reptile cousins. The ancestors of primates must have escaped from better equipped mammalians and the ancestors of humans must have escaped from better equipped primates.

Man, in fact, is the product of neither fallen angels nor risen apes. Man stems from fallen apes. The Bible is more accurate than science in its explanation of the origin of human life. Our ancestors, our Adams and Eves, were evicted from Paradise. The truth is that they were not evicted by Almighty God, but by better equipped or fitter apes.

By the close of the Miocene era, our ancestors were living in the savannah, about to confront the Pliocene epoch, which lasted 13-1 million years ago. This was the most testing time in the history of mankind - an era of climatic deteriorations and droughts which transformed Africa into a graveyard for many species. This climatically aggressive situation left a deep scar on the human brain, a scar which must have influenced the mind in its creation of the first idea of hell. It says, in the Sumerian epic "Inanna's Journey to Hell": " Here is no water but only rock, rock and no water and the sandy road ".....

In "The Epic of Gilgamesh" the writer states that "Hell is frightening because of its sandy dust"... It is " the river which has no water."

In order to escape from the woodlands into the savannah, our ancestors must have been more undeveloped than the rest of the apes.

Even today, most scientists agree that we are in a phase of infancy or neoteny. "The characteristic which is so vital for the peculiarity of true man, that of always remaining in a state of development, is quite certainly a gift we owe to the neotenous nature of mankind, " writes K. Lorenz.

To be in a "state of development" one has to be in an undeveloped state. In fact, even today, an adult human being looks more like an infant chimpanzee than an adult chimpanzee. Our ancestors may have never developed canine teeth. Had we had stronger innate drives we might

3

have never developed our big brain.

Life in the savannah produced one important change in the evolution of our species: the enlargement of the brain.

The permanent frustration caused by the new environment of the savannah produced a constant pressure on our ancestors' brain cells, causing their growth and an increase in the volume of the human brain. Irritation is one of the major causes of expansion and growth in nature.

By carrying an increase in frustration, each escape contributed to the increase in the volume of the brain. The reptilian brain is bigger than that of fishes, the mammalian bigger than that of reptiles, the primate's bigger than that of the rest of the mammals and the human brain is bigger than that of primates.

In reality we have three brains which are interconnected. They can also behave independently sometimes. We have the old brain representing our reptilian past, we have the limbic brain representing our mammalian legacy and we have the new brain, which is particularly developed in our species and which we inherit from our primate ancestors.

Each of these brains has its own anatomy, its own chemistry, its own rationality and reasoning, its own values and its own attitudes and behaviour.

Frustrations, irritations and fears played the main role in the expansion of our brains.

The aim of the development of any new brain was the reduction of frustration, irritation or fears of the previous brain.

By developing learning and memory, the limbic brain helps to placate or to reduce the frustration, irritations or fears of the reptilian brain, which, operating on the here and now short term basis, has difficulty to learn that many things which at first sight are frightening, are not dangerous in reality.

By developing sociality, gregariousness and the group life, the limbic brain reduced the fears of loneliness of the reptilian existence.

Vocalization and hearing, these important attributes of the limbic brain, help communication and the mobilization of group defenses, or group prevention of danger.

4

With the superior level of the limbic brain, which is particularly well developed in our species, we developed the typically humane characteristics such as: sympathy, empathy, friendship, cuddling, sharing, nursing, nurturing and taking care of the old. All of these placate or reduce a great deal of our frustrations, irritations or fears.

With our big new brain we acquired the ability to reason ourselves out of frustrations, irritations or fears.

The relationship between fears and our three brains is evident whenever our new brain cannot reason us out of a fear and whenever our limbic brain is unable to cope with that fear, we return to our reptilian brain and its reasoning and values. The stronger the fear or irritation, the more prominent the reptilian legacy.

Whenever our limbic brain and our new brain are reduced in efficiency by alcohol, drugs, stress, disease, old age, a fervent belief, a fixed prejudice, or an infatuation, our reasoning, attitudes and behaviour become influenced by our reptilian inheritance. Infants who have not developed, or those who will never develop, the organization of the limbic brain and the new brain are also influenced by their reptilian brains.

The main characteristics of the reptilian brain's behaviour are: selfishness, self-centredness, ruthlessness, treachery, viciousness, suspicion, callousness, cruelty, cold-bloodedness, rigidity, stubbornness, perseverance, individual rivalry and competition, individual assertiveness, territoriality, distance, impatience, intolerance, aggression and violence, poor care for infants, here and now utilitarian opportunism and gratification and the care of appearance.

The reptilian brain also rules ritualistic stereo-type behaviour. Eliminating the efficiency of our new brain and our limbic brain, stress or lasting fear forces us towards compulsive obsessions which are in tune with the reptilian legacy.

The reptilian brain becomes evident with the attitudes and behaviour of obtuse or autistic children, children who do not develop the organization of their limbic brain and particularly of their humane brain.

Under stress or frustration we might pick our noses or scratch our heads, all ruled by our reptilian legacy.

When under threat, a reptilian usually assumes a posture of defiance, a display aiming to impress the enemy by inflating his body or part of it.

Our obsession with status symbolism, with decorations, with a boasting of our importance through gadgets, opulence, luxury goods or tattoos are all in tune with our reptilian legacy which takes over whenever we feel threatened and we feel threatened mostly in our pretensions and in our over-ambitions. With pretensions and over-ambitions we develop the fear that we might not achieve them.

Military uniforms, particularly those of high ranking officers, with epaulettes and impressive hats, were created under the influence of our reptilian brain. Military parades remind us of the reptilian behaviour. The military " goose step" should be renamed the "reptilian step". Military decorations fit the reptilian tendency to impress when frightened.

In the reptilian species, hierarchy and rank play a dominant role. Like other mammals or primates, we exhibit our hierarchical rank whenever we are intimidated or frightened.

Reptilians fear touch; they keep their distance. It is this innate drive which makes reptilians territorial animals. In fact, like other mammalians or primates, we become territorial when threatened.

When a reptilian has been beaten by an adversary , or when it has lost its territory, it becomes depressed and impotent. Many humans when beaten by a rival or when they have lost their wealth, which to them is a kind of dominion, a kind of territory, easily return to their reptilian existence.

The mammalian or the limbic brain evolved around the reptilian brain under the pressure of the reptilian brain's frustrations, irritations and fears.

The limbic brain's main abilities are: sociality, gregariousness, family and group life, care for infants, curiosity and exploration, learning and memory, vocalization and hearing, communication and play, touch and intimacy. All of these reduce frustrations, irritations and fears.

With its centres for communication and language, the

limbic brain helps to achieve a calming intimacy and togetherness among the members of a community. When we are under a strong fear or on drugs we lose the efficiency of our limbic system, so we return to reptilian body language.

With the limbic brain's sociality, reptilian violent and ruthless individual competition or rivalry are replaced by individual cooperation, by a community life. Intraspecific fights among mammalians are far less violent than reptilian ones. The mammalian territoriality is a reptilian legacy which comes into prominence when threatened or frightened.

The limbic brain is the brain of emotions which helps it to develop learning and memory. Memorisation of events and the revocation of past experiences from the memory pool are activities. Activities are ruled by energy. In fact it is emotions which provide the extra energy to operate the memory's activities. Mobilising our hormonal system and the autonomous nervous system, emotions create extra nervous energy. Impressive events create stronger biochemical arousals, stronger emotions and stronger emotions create deeper memories.

Every experience is accompanied by an emotion. Each experience, in fact, is registered in our memory pool on its own specific frequency of emotional energy. For example, episodes that occured in a state of drunkenness will be remembered more vividly on the same level of drunkenness.

When the limbic brain loses its efficiency under stress or fear and when the reptilian brain comes into prominence, we lose our memory.

The limbic brain's learning and memory reduce fears as they help one to realise that not everything is always a life-threatening danger.

Curiosity, play and trial and error flexible exploration, typical of the limbic brain, all help enrich the memory.

Learning and memory reduce much reptilian violence, rapaciousness and brusqueness and above all the urgent here and now gratification.

Learning and memory create a notion of time.

The limbic brain brings less stubborn and less persevering behaviour in changing conditions, opening the way to more flexible and more adaptable behaviour. Reptilian predictability is replaced by the limbic brain's improvisation.

With the limbic brain and its developed centres of vision and hearing, a safer information about the environment and a wider participation in life becomes available. This reduces the unknown and the fear of it. Reptilian contact to the external world is more limited as it is made mainly through smell and taste.

Sociality, cooperation and mothering which are related to the limbic brain are needs of this brain in the same way as ruthless selfishness and violent competition are the needs of the reptilian brain. When animals or humans with a well developed limbic brain risk their lives to protect their offspring, it is not out of altruism, but of the gratification of a need of the limbic brain. A distress signal from an infant triggers off the centre of the need for caring and protecting the infant. What we interpret as a mother's sacrifice for her infant in reality can be considered as a gratification of the mother's need for caring and protection which was stimulated by the infant's distress signal.

These needs of the limbic brain, so acutely developed in humans, create a nervous arousal which we call emotion. It is this emotion which creates the nervous energy needed for the activities involved to gratify the needs of the limbic brain.

The main difference between reptilian and limbic brains is that the drives of the former are inherited, operating automatically and instantly as conditioned reflexes, while the potential of the latter has to be developed through exercise and experience in early infancy in order to be operative and efficient.

Mammalians, primates and humans are born with the nueronal mass of the limbic brain, but in order to have an efficient limbic system this mass of the limbic brain's cells has to be formed and structured. This is done mainly through experiences and learning in early infancy. If the limbic brain has not developed its needs for sociality and togetherness, for communication and speech, for caring and mothering, in infancy, it has difficulty in developing them later.

8

A child is born a selfish, self-centred, ruthless reptilian and he will remain dominated by the mechanism of the reptilian brain for the rest of his life if in his early infancy his mother and the community have not taught him the valuable potential of the limbic brain. Obtuseness and autism are the best examples of the validity of my theory, as these are obvious consequences of an undeveloped limbic brain's organisation.

When a well developed organisation of the limbic brain has been shaken by deep stress, terror, severe illness or drugs, the reptilian brain takes over.

Due to the fragility, vulnerability and fears of our species, we developed a superior layer of limbic brain which I will call, the humane brain, with its centres and needs for dealing with typically humane feelings and behaviour such as: friendship, affection, pity , sympathy, empathy, compassion, gentleness, sharing and caring for the sick, the young and the old.

This exceptional development of our limbic brain was somehow stimulated by the particular frustrations and fears our ancestors had to face in the African savannah. Without any specialisation and without the inborn natural offensive or defensive weapons, our species had to compete for its survival with more specialized and dangerous animals. In fact, we must have been the most pathetic species, omnivorous scavengers, living in big groups for protective reasons.

Our highly developed limbic brain enabled us to understand others and their feelings. Without this understanding, reptilian self-love would have never become love or loving, without this understanding there would never have been sympathy or empathy, pity or compassion, sharing or kindness.

This theory can be proved by the fact that when the superior layers of our limbic brain are damaged or shaken in their efficiency by drugs or strong fears, our humaneness is reduced or even disappears.

This humane brain also contains needs such as gratitude. a sense of humour and laughter.

Like the limbic brain, its superior layers must be

developed in early infancy. Once developed, these centres of the humane brain develop the urge or craving to be active. By gratifying these needs we reach contentment and joyfulness.

When we develop the humane brain's centre for loving, we develop the need for loving and contentment when we gratify this need, when we love. There is no love without a need for loving. The humane brain craves a need for being needed. In fulfiling this need we feel to have achieved a fuller and safer existence.

Confronted with an invalid, the needy, or helpless children, someone with a developed humane brain will feel the need to do something to help and he will feel satisfied and content as a result of the gratification of the humane brain's needs. On the other hand, a person dominated by the reptilian brain will take advantage of these people, ruthlessly exploiting them.

Stimulating one of the centres or needs of the humane brain, triggers off the activities of other centres of the same brain. Loving people become more sympathetic and friendly and ready to help those in need. Triggering off the centre of the sense of humour or that of laughter, easily triggers off centres such as generosity. In fact, charities collecting money for those in need are more successful if organised by comedians or entertainers. Caring for a pet makes us more humane in relation to humans and nature. In fact, owning a pet is good exercise for the humane brain. Exercising our humane brain brings serenity, the best prevention against many diseases.

By developing the humane brain, we develop a further and wider participation in life, a keener learning and memory and a reduced lack of comprehension and memory in old age. By cultivating our humane brain, we develop better understanding and sympathy, which widens relationships and togetherness.

By operating with the humane brain, we achieve maturity. With maturity we reach true freedom, freedom from fear. This is why maturity implies serenity and wisdom.

Using the humane brain creates an invigorating well-being which rejuvenates health and energy, thus creating fruitfulness, fecundity, magnanimity and the joy of living.

The main function of our neo-cortex, or new brain, was to help us reason ourselves out of our fears and frustrations and by analysing fearful events in order to dedramatise them.

This new brain also helped our ancestors to adapt to the ever-changing environment. It helped us to compensate for our lack of inborn tools and weapons with artificially made ones.

If our ancestors in the savannah had been better equipped by nature or with specialisation, we would never have become "Homo faber" and even less " Homo sapiens". But, as I stressed earlier, if the ancestors of our ancestors had been better equipped by nature we would never have left the woodlands in the first place.

Many scientists agree that even the other primates use their new brains in a more complex problem solving and that the difference between them and us is only a matter of degrees as far as mental activity is concerned. We consider other primates inferior, however, as they are not able to have an abstract or speculative wishful way of thinking.

In my view, the most significant difference between other primates and us is that while other primates' new brains work in harmony and collaboration with their limbic brains, our new brain often operates independently from our limbic brain, sometimes even against it. This is perhaps due, to the fact that in other primates the limbic brain is stronger, better developed and more mature, therefore does not allow an independent activity of the neo-cortex.

In its independent activity our new brain developed abstractions, fantasies, illusions, day-dreams and wishful beliefs.

We are born with the new brain poorly harmonized with our limbic system. In fact, children's independent activity or the fantasizing of the new brain is well known.

Inspired by innate playfulness, the new brain starts playing with itself creating an unreal world of imagination. Growing up, which implies development of the organization of our limbic brain, the brain reflecting reality, the independent activity of the new brain becomes more under the control of our limbic brain. It is as if the connections between the two brains become firmer.

With mental maturity which coincides with a fully developed organization of the limbic brain, independent activity or fantasizing of the new brain becomes limited.

We have three phases as far as the independent activity of the new brain is concerned. We have infancy in which the limbic brain is not yet properly developed as to be able to control the new brain fantasizing. The playful nature of infants plays with the fantasy world of the new brain.

In maturity the connection between the limbic and the new brains are less loose so we do not take our fantasies seriously either.

In the intermediary phase of adolescence, however, we take ourselves and our wishful beliefs seriously.

It is in this phase that we invent faith which we put into our wishful beliefs. Our faith which keeps our wishful belief alive, blinds us as it reduces the efficiency of our sense, our perception and our common sense reasoning.

It is in this phase that we create our mind with its wishful world which then becomes our supreme ruler.

The mind is thus the creation of an independent new brain, a brain which has escaped from the control of the limbic brain, the brain which represents our contact with reality. The lesser the limbic brain is developed, the stronger the independent activity of the new brain, the richer is its fantasy world. Extreme independent activity of the new brain is evident in those suffering from schizophrenia.

Any weakening of the limbic system through alcohol, drugs or fear and the loosening of its connection with the new brain, increases the fantasies and wishful speculations of the new brain.

Many people call the mind's world our inner nature. Instead it is more super-nature, a world created by a mental disorder. We are even proud to be the only animals able to live in the world of abstractions. We often call our wishful fantasies or hallucinations, revelations.

Having better developed limbic and humane brains, woman is generally less influenced by the world of the mind than man.

With the appearance of the mind a major change took

place in the life of our species. Instead of being ruled by our common sense intelligence, our behaviour and attitudes became influenced by the mind's wishful beliefs, ideologies, superstitions, or prejudices.

The difference between the two is that while common sense intelligence has its limits which seldom allow excessiveness or irrationality, behaviour inspired by the mind tends to expand resulting in over-expansion or catastrophic excess. The mind invented its own rationality, its own logic and its own values.

The power of the mind is so strong that it is able to choose from the memory and from past experiences only those episodes which help wishful expectations and the pretentiousness of the given moment. In the mind's world, the proverb " Out of sight, out of mind", would be more accurate if reversed: "Out of mind, out of sight."

The stronger the mind's wishful beliefs or prejudices, the stronger its narrow-mindedness, the stronger our insensitivity becomes.

Many people might say: "So, what? What's wrong living in a world of fantasies, what's wrong taking wishful beliefs and ideologies seriously ? "

The wrong is that living in the precarious world of the mind we acquire new fears, fears that our wishful beliefs and illusions might not be fulfiled, that they might be derided by reality. By creating wishful beliefs the mind also creates enemies of those beliefs, their menacing antitheses, their devils.

What is even more tragic, as our wishful beliefs and hopeful ideologies are lasting, often a permanent frame of mind, we acquire lasting anxieties, permanent fears which may be a serious peril to our mental and physical health. It is in the mind's world that we find the source of our main psychosomatic diseases and mental disorders.

The stronger our escape into the world of the mind, the greater is our precariousness, the bigger are our anxieties and fears. Extreme escape is accompanied by fears of paranoiac dimensions.

Another even greater wrong is that the mind's created fears brought us millions of years back in evolutionary terms: they brought us back to our cold-blooded, ruthless, selfish and self-centred reptilian existence. In fact, many of our mental disorders can be said to be due to excessive reptilian behaviour.

In its expansion the mind's belief can reach its extreme: fanaticism. This brings the extreme reptilian legacy into prominence. In its servile devotion to its abstract belief, fanaticism is capable of murder, of killing even members of its own family.

The world of the mind is a world of discontent. Like any other creation of the mind, discontent tends to expand. It tends to expand because the mind tries to solve its problems by escaping into higher and more remote wishful beliefs, which increase precariousness and discontent. This is why beliefs and ideologies, prejudices and speculations tend to over-expand and in their over-expansion they reach nightmares.

In my view, a radical change in the evolution of the human mind took place with the agricultural revolution which started some ten thousand years ago.

Agriculture and the domestication of animals must have been discovered by women. In general women have better developed limbic and humane brains. Only brains which possess centres of caring, nursing and loving could have started cultivating plants and fruit. Only women could have had the idea of domesticating animals: nurturing is in women's nature. In the first mythologies the main divinities of agriculture were women.

With agriculture and the domestication of animals, man acquired leisure time. Previously, food gathering must have been a full time activity.

During this leisure time, man, particularly in the adolescent phase, extended the fantasizing of his new brain. The more free time we have, the more we day-dream. Falling in love with the fantasies of his mind, man rejected maturity preferring to remain with his adolescent mentality. What is more, maturity implies responsibility, a caring way of reasoning against which male adolescence tends to rebel. In the fantasy of his mind, the male adolescent invented the wishful belief or desire of being superior to woman, which

14

represented reality or nature and he placed the weight of his aggressive faith into this belief. In the precariousness and fear that wishful beliefs carry, man found the necessary energy for his aggression.

In the Sahara art of ten thousand years ago, we can see for the first time in the history of mankind some mythical figures inspired by the fantasy of man's mind, appearing.

Man became intoxicated by his mind and its wishful way of reasoning. His mind placed him at the centre of the universe, above nature and reality. Self-conceit and self-deceit were born.

I think that man's wishful desire to rise above nature was inspired by women's successful agricultural revolution and her success in the domestication of animals.

What man never understood is the fact that the agricultural revolution and the domestication of animals were achieved by women's humane brain's ability to co-operate with nature. In his arrogant mind, man started and perpetuated his stubborn adolescent belief that he too could dominate or subdue nature by forcing it to adapt or co-operate with his pretentious beliefs. Man is pursuing this stubborn belief in spite of evidence that his attitude is causing such a disastrous ecological crisis.

Fanatic believers thrive on self-deceit. They are easily seduced by flatteries. A believer is not " Homo sapiens " he is " Homo credulus ".

Self-conceit and self-deceit brought a uniqueness in nature: ridicule. Ridicule basically consists of the mind's taking itself and its abstract speculations seriously.

The mind reaches its extreme ridicule when it tries to solve its problem of doubt in its belief by expanding the belief, by becoming fanatical about it. In its fanaticism the mind is able to reach its extreme conceit: belief in miracles, which are contrary to the basic laws of reality and nature. This is when extreme ridicule reaches extreme pathos.

We are proud to stress that we are the only species able to laugh. We seldom mention, however, that we are also the only laughable species. Other animals are only laughable when they imitate us or when they remind us of our pretensions.

Wishful reasoning of the mind produced wishful

beliefs, wishful ideologies, wishful prejudices and wishful · fixed ideas. Man started leaning on them, he started being ruled and guided by them. Man placed himself above nature in the world of the mind's super-nature. In reality, laughter mainly occurs when those living in the world of super-nature crash down into the real world of nature. This is why believers persecute laughter.

Placing himself above nature, man resorted to prayers: man became a beggar. With prayer he started appealing to super-natural forces to force nature to suit his wishful caprices and even cried when his wishful caprices had problems in becoming reality.

The world of the mind soon became an intoxication, an addiction. Like any addiction the mind's addiction quickly spread, becoming a culture, the culture of humanity. We live in a culture of the mind's addictions. We are so drugged by our culture that we do not accept the existence of any other life, of any other reasoning, of any other values. Like drug addicts the mind's addicts consider those who reach maturity and sobriety as inferior. Our present intoxicating culture glorifies activities in the field of abstraction and fiction, philosophising and poeticizing. Our present culture prevents humanity from evolving from the adolescent male mentality into maturity, humaneness and maternity.

Every one of us possesses "animus" and " anima" , male and female characteristics, as C, Jung says. In reality, each of us has the ability to reason either with the mind more in tune with the adolescent male mentality, or with the humane brain which implies a mature mentality, which is maternal in its nature.

Many insist that we have an innate drive, an instinct for religious and ideological beliefs. If this was true, it would be a joke of nature. It would be a joke because it would mean that nature had provided us with an instinct placing us in a ridiculous situation. The ridiculous does not belong to nature, it is part of super-nature. Nature cannot create super-nature because this would be an even bigger joke as super-nature's supreme aim is to destroy, deform or subdue nature.

But, even if nature had endowed us with the capacity to create fantasies and myths, nature would never have entitled us to take them seriously.

The mind's world is a world of precariousness and instability. It is the world of anxieties and fears. The mind's wishful beliefs or expectations carry anxieties and fears that they might not be realised or fulfilled. These anxieties and fears produce a nervous energy which creates a state of tension or a state of arousal.

We started liking this tension. This mind created tension gives us an impression of living more intensively, more fully. Being an illusion of the mind, this tension reduces the efficiency of our senses and of our perception thereby limiting our participation in reality, in life.

We become addicted to the mind's created tension, often calling it excitement. We are so obsessed with excitement that we spend most of our lives in pursuit of it.

We thrive on these exciting arousals because they reduce the efficiency of our senses and our perception.

Reducing the efficiency of our senses and of our perceptions, excitements render us insensitive to reality. A pretentious mind finds reality dull or boring because it threatens its infatuation, because it does not take its pretentiousness or its assumed seriousness, seriously.

The real nature of excitement is evident when observing people watching a competitive match. We seldom watch a match if we are not intensely interested in one of the players or teams. The apprehension or dread that our preferred team might lose, mobilises our autonomous nervous system and our adrenalin, creating a tension or an arousal which we consider excitement. In fact, the more we support one of the competitors, the more excited we are by the match.

It is this fear that our team might lose that provides the energy needed to go to the match, applaud and encourage our team and to insult the adversary.

That excitements are caused by anxieties or fears can be deduced from the fact that in both cases we have higher blood pressure, a higher level of adrenalin in the blood, in both cases we often sweat and tremble, all resulting in a reduction in the efficiency of our senses, our perception and our reasoning.

Due to the worries about the unpredictability of a trip abroad, we might feel a " Reise Fieber ", travel sickness, nausea or drowsiness. A predictable or safe trip is positively less exciting.

High anxieties like high excitement can produce ecstasy, euphoria as well as stupor or fainting.

Other significant inventions of the mind in search of excitement through anxieties or fears are horror films, criminal literature or threatening ugliness in modern art or adventurous science-fiction stories.

Another excitement that our mind created is music. Distorting the harmony of nature, man-made music inspires a certain anxiety which also provides excitement.

Evidence that most man-made music is frightening is that it frightens animals, sometimes to the point of panic. The Ancient Greek story claiming that Orpheus charmed animals with his lute, is a myth. Animals are, after all, frightened by noises of other animals as most of them represent a lament or a distress signal caused by biochemical irritation or fear. An animal in distress is a source of potential danger.

Many people might ask what is wrong living for excitements? Firstly, much of our present ecological crisis, endangering all forms of life on our planet, is due to our irrational pursuit of excitement. Secondly, the pursuit of excitement is dangerous to our physical and mental health. With anxieties or excitements some of our body's neurotransmitters inhibit the activity of our immune system, exposing us to many opportunistic infections, infections which prosper when our immune defenses are reduced. In fact, we are the unhealthiest species compared to any other species, not to mention our wide variety of mental disorders, another peculiarity of our species. Thirdly, excitement always brings post-excitement exhaustion, gloom and depression. In these states we are desperate for more excitements which are often not available or are difficult to find. In fact, we are a deeply depressed species, otherwise why do we turn to stimulants, drugs, etc in order to "fix"

18

this depression. Fourthly, life dedicated to excitement stops us from achieving the serenity of maturity.

The myth of "Peter Pan" would be more accurate if applied to the adolescent man trying to avoid reaching maturity. For an adolescent man, excitements are more amusing than maturity's serenity and sobriety.

Peterpanism is a man's phenomenon. It is impossible to imagine a Mary Pan, as most girls aspire to become mothers, which implies maturity.

Let's not forget that man is the only animal capable of retaining his adolescent mentality after having reached biological adulthood.

In order to ensure people to remain insensitive to social or economic problems, the authorities often organize thrills and excitements by providing celebrations, games, festivals or ceremonies: at times even international tension, or war.

The mind created its own culture. This consists of cults of wishful speculations such as beliefs and ideologies, illusions and mirages, day-dreams and fantasies, myths and superstitions.

This mind's culture places wishful revelations on an altar. The sacred transforms a believer into a devotee. Devotion blinds us. It can make us insensitive even to physical pain. Ignoring physical pain is a danger to health and survival. The mind's main purpose, however, is not our physical survival, but its own survival.

Our mind's culture does not illuminate us, it intoxicates us. In this state of intoxication we serve our culture like drugged dependents. Even our bloody revolutions or wars do not serve to eliminate the mind's world of beliefs and ideologies but merely replace them with new beliefs and ideologies.

Like any other addiction, our culture's aim is to perpetuate itself by spreading itself, by expanding.

The mind has an advantage over maturity and wisdom. The mind's wishful beliefs always carry the fear that they might not be realised. This provides an extra nervous energy which serves the believer's audacity and aggression. Having a lesser developed limbic brain than woman, man inclines to escape deeper into the world of abstract fantasies and wishful beliefs than woman. This places him in a higher precariousness and fears, providing him with an extra nervous energy, which he uses to impose himself over woman, in his aggression against her. Man's higher precariousness and fear can easily be deduced by his greater selfishness and self-centredness, the levels of which are directly related to the levels of his precariousness and fears.

Man also uses this extra nervous energy to propagate or expand his aggressive culture based on fantasies and wishful beliefs, a culture in which women's maturity and humaneness are ignored or denigrated. This man-made culture, which denigrates the achievements of evolution, creates a life of tension and fears. In fact, our present culture creates far more discontent and agitation than happiness or a joy of living.

The culture of fantasies and wishful beliefs, which provides extra nervous energy, could not but create a neurotic life.

IDEALIZED SELF

Discontented with our real self, reflected in our limbic brain, the mind invented its own self, an idealized wishful self, an ego. Man often organizes his whole life around his wishful ego. He is able to sacrifice the very survival of his real self for the status, fame or glory of his idealized self. In fact , in many cases of suicide, practiced only by our species, we have a pretentious mind's self, hating and eliminating the real self.

We pompously called this idealized self our personal identity. Some people spend a great deal of their lives in search of this identity.

Being a wishful abstraction created by a pretentious mind, personal identity tends to expand with the expansion of the mind's pretentiousness and expectations, often ending in mental disorder.

A self-created self is out of reality. Like any other abstraction, a self-made self takes itself seriously. Like any other abstraction a self-made self tends to expand resulting in over-seriousness, which is not serious as it is the source of ridicule.

Leaning on an invented ego creates precariousness. This carries fears. We develop a terrible fear that our wishful self might become a failure. This fear brings our reptilian brain into prominence. Our wishful ego can reach extreme selfishness and self-centredness and ruthless self-interest. The more our ego is inflated, the more reptilian characteristics emerge.

Like any other mind's abstraction, a wishful ego craves to become reality. More and more people insist that there is a sacred human right, a right to self-fulfilment, another source of ridicule.

Self-fulfilment, which in essence consists of the insertion into reality of an idealized wishful self, which by its very nature is above the abilities and merits of the real self, can only be realized on the expenses of nature or at the expense of others.

Craving to become reality , an ego is aggressive. In fact, self-fulfilment or self-assertion imply forcing reality or other people to adapt to the pretensions of a capricious self-made wishful self. This creates aggression against natural order and against the community in the name of the selfish ego.

We can visualize the absurdity of the mind's idea of self-fulfilment if we imagine a situation in which everyone succeeded in realising his idealised self. The picture would be even more grotesque if those who believe in their " inner divine essence" realised their self-created divinities.

In the USA where self-assertion is a supreme cult, a kind of constitutional right, many advise "assertiveness therapy" as the best cure against depression, a depression which, in reality, is often caused by the cult of self-assertion.

Those advising this cure forget that successful self-assertion creates victims. Living among victims emarginates the successful, forcing him to live in loneliness which is the usual source of depression.

What is more, successful self-assertion increases the ego's pretensions which increases discontent and anxieties. A pretentious person is never content as it is in the nature of pretentiousness to become more pretentious, to expand with any new fulfilment.

With the mind's self-made wishful self our self-awareness came into existence. With self- awareness subjectivity and objectivity were born; two worlds apart, two worlds in conflict as the former developed fear of the latter. This fear must have inspired the Judeo-Christian mind to invent a God who entitled man to be superior to the external world and to dominate it, in accordance with the wishfulness of his pretentious mind and the mind's inflated ego.

In this relationship between the subjective and the objective, objectivity cannot but be subjective, a wishful speculation able to gratify the mind's needs.

We usually fall in love with our idealised self which reduces the efficiency of our senses, of our perception and of our reasoning even more.

In narcissism, in which man reaches extreme self-love, he also reaches extreme insensitivity and insensibility.

Most of man's life is spent performing a role inspired by his mind's ego.

Guided by her common sense intelligence and a superior sense of adaptation, woman usually adapts herself, or pretends to adapt to man's role. In fact, our present life is that of a tragicomedy, a tragi-comic performance. Performance produces performance anxiety or stage fright. This creates a chain of stress-related diseases and mental disorders so characteristic of our species in its existence dominated by the male adolescent mentality.

On the stage human communications are reduced. Those playing a role concentrate mainly on their own lines and this limits hearing and perception of external information.

Our life is a life of monologues. We act for our own sake, for the sake of our ego. Being fragile, our wishful ego needs constant encouragement or flattery.

The life of the theatre is a life of facades. Behind the life of facades hides a sad life of secrecy.

Identifying himself and his life with his ego, his ego's status or facade, man becomes highly fragile, because an inflated ego is easily deflated. An ego's failure can be a real tragedy: it can provoke impotence, sterility, depression or suicide. This is best seen with people who identify their egos with their jobs. Losing their jobs they are lost. Unemployment exposes many people to heart failure, high blood pressure, over-weight, depression and all kind of opportunistic infections.

AGGRESSION

With the appearance of the mind, the ugliest of our characteristics loomed: offensive and destructive aggression.

The mind's abstract wishful beliefs crave materialisation and this is mainly realized by forcing objective reality and its natural order to fit or to adapt to the mind's abstractions. This implies aggression aiming at the destruction of this reality.

This mind's destructive aggression is best observed when its beliefs or ideologies reach fanaticism. There is no peace or tolerance in the mind's world. Abstract wishful beliefs and ideologies are impregnated with restlessness, agitation, hostility and militancy. The mind creates partisans with the motto " Who is not with me, is against me".

The mind is opinionated which implies stubborn offensiveness.

There are two main views regarding the origin of man's aggression. To Instinctivists, our aggressiveness is phylogenetically programmed, an instinct. For this school of thought life is a jungle in which the fittest, whatever that may mean, has a better chance of survival and of transmitting his aggressive genes to the following generations. To Behaviourists, human aggression is mainly caused by social and cultural environments.

There is even a tendency to link these two extremes by explaining that our aggressiveness is a result of the interaction of our environments, with inherited genes.

These theories are in accord with the adolescent mentality, a mentality which seeks to excuse an individual's selfish and self-centred behaviour: Instinctivists blaming nature, Behaviourists blaming the environment.

Some representatives of the instinct theory claim that our aggression is highly beneficial. In his book " On Aggression", Konrad Lorenz wrote: "Summing up what has been said in this chapter, we find that aggression, far from being the diabolic destructive principle that classical psychoanalysis makes it out to be, is really an essential part of life, preserving the organisation of instincts."

24

Those, like Lorenz, playing with the idea of instinct often do not realize that they are playing with a myth which is able to explain everything but itself.

What is more, those who consider human aggression as beneficiary should ask the victims of this aggression for their opinion.

In Spengler's "Man and Techniques" we read the following : "The beast of prey is the highest form of active life...The human race ranks highly because it belongs to the class of the beast of prey"...... "the life of a man is the life of a brave and splendid, cruel and cunning beast of prey. He lives by catching, killing and consuming. Since he exists he must be master."

In Bertrand Russell's "Authority and the Individual", we read: "The old instincts that have come down to us from our tribal ancestors, all kinds of aggressive impulses inherited from generations of savages"....

I would like to point out to those who insist that man was and is a born "hunter and killer", that nature would never have given the predatory instinct to a species with the digestive system of a vegetarian, like other primates. If man was a "beast of prey" he would never have started agriculture, the domestication of animals and the dairy industry.

Man's inflated ego cannot but see his past in heroic terms.

It would have been a joke of nature to give man the instinct to hunt and to kill without also giving him an inborn, natural weapon to enable him to do so. Man has no innate offensive or defensive weapons. He had to invent and only very recently (some 10 to 15 thousand years ago) artificial, man-made weapons enabling him to hunt and to kill.

Our pretentious mind's culture invented the myth of "Man the Hunter". For millions of years we were pathetic food gatherers in the African savannah, competing with much better equipped predators and scavengers. Man is not a hunter by nature, he is a rapist of nature, an unscrupulous vandaliser of its order. Our present ecological crisis is evidence of this.

There might be a clearer understanding of the subject

if we analysed the origin and nature of the energy that is needed for human aggressiveness to materialise.

As I have explained, the brain and the nervous system of both animals and humans are programmed to increase the energy in their bodies in cases of emergency such as when they have to defend their survival or the survival of their offspring and when they have to satisfy their needs inspired by biological discomforts, such as hunger, thirst and sex. In nature, aggression is either a defence against an objective threat, or a reaction to fears caused by physiological imbalance or discomfort. In both cases the extra energy is provided by biological arousals created by real fears.

Humans, however, also possess the mind's generated aggression which is offensive.

Offensive aggressiveness is mainly inspired by our inflated ego's fear of failure.

Like a realistic danger to physical survival, any positive or imaginary threat to our ego, or to the survival of our mind's world, creates an emergency state of existence. In emotional arousals, produced by this state of emergency, offensive aggressiveness finds the energy which helps its materialisation, the energy for its destructiveness.

Why is offensive aggression destructive?

Because the main threat to the adolescent mind's ego and its imaginary world is nature, objective reality. There is only one way to protect our mind's world against nature and that is by changing it to please our mind. Moulding nature to suit the wishful abstractions of our mind results in destroying nature.

Neither Instinctivists nor Behaviourists realise the strength of the mind, or the aggression inspired by it. Our mind's infatuations, prejudices and beliefs are far stronger than our genes or environment. Our physical self-preservation is secondary to the preservation of our inflated ego.

Most crimes of violence and destruction are premeditated. The mind's created imagination or speculations, beliefs or prejudices play an essential role in premeditation.

The following facts could help in proving that the

26

origin of our destructive aggression lies in our minds.

Ablation of the frontal lobe where the wishful way of thinking seems to take place, reduces offensive aggressiveness.

Offensive aggression can be manipulated by influencing the mind with propaganda or brain-washing.

In order to arouse aggressiveness in their followers, political and military leaders depict their opponents as monsters, criminals or dangerous war-mongers. Conflicts are carried on by the energy provided by fears of defeat and fears of defeat by "monsters" increase emotional arousals and aggression even more.

Hysterical delirium of the masses, created by the manipulation of their minds, can lead to the most atrocious destruction and savagery.

Terrorism is inspired mainly by belief.

When the mind becomes obsessed by a belief or an idea, it develops fanaticism, a serious cause of barbaric destructions.

Tyranny, this epitome of offensive aggression, is always based on a belief or an ideology. Cruelty is a product of the mind's prejudices or beliefs.

One of the worst types of offensive aggression can be found in persecutions or revolutions and these are inspired by an idea or a belief.

Other major instigators of crime and violence are racial or national prejudices, all creations of the mind. People inspired by these prejudices often justify their killings with the belief that they are not eliminating members of their own species, other human beings, but 'barbarians' or "Undermenschen".

Jealousy, envy, vanity, resentment, malice, despise and spitefulness are all sources of offensive aggression and are all states of mind, or emotions created by states of mind.

The real nature of destructive aggression lies in hatred. Hatred belongs to the mind's world of beliefs. There is no hatred in the animal world or in humans when in their mature phase.

Vindictiveness, which is a serious source of offensive and destructive aggression, is a creation of the mind and its ego.

"There is no love without aggression" stressed Lorenz. This is very true, but only in those with the adolescent mentality. Their love, in fact, is self-love and this is aggressive.

Throughout time and space, the torture of man by man has been committed in the name of a belief or a prejudice. Inquisitors are always ardent believers.

Man considers a moral insult a good reason for strong reaction. But insults stem from excessive self-esteem.

Some people insist that frustration is at the root of most of our offensive aggression. Frustration, however, is nothing but self-infatuation offended by reality. We are frustrated in a bus or train full of what we consider ugly and ordinary people, or working in a crowded office or factory. We are not frustrated, however, by a much bigger gathering at a reception at Buckingham Palace or the White House, or a fashionable night club. Man is seldom frustrated by the crowd in which he feels important, that is applauding him, carrying him on their shoulders or pressing him for his autograph.

Self-confidence is another significant source of destructive aggression.

It is important to stress that self-confidence is usually preceded by self-righteousness, a wishful belief. In fact, self-confidence finds the energy needed for its materialization in the fear that self-righteousness might not be realized.

The glorification of self-confidence invaded Western Europe with the Renaissance. "It is better to be adventurous than cautious," wrote Machiavelli, "because fortune is like a woman and if you wish to keep her under, it is necessary to beat and ill-use her."Machiavelli certainly did not know that self-confidence in a life ruled by uncertainty and unpredictability ends in a stubbornness derided by ironies. Corneille was much wiser when, in his "Cid" he explained that "Danger breeds best on too much confidence."

One of the main evidences, however, that offensive and destructive aggression belongs to the male adolescent mentality dominated by the wishful speculations of the mind, is that women, who are less influenced by abstract speculations and more by the humane brain, practice this aggression far less.

Those women who imitate men, who are infatuated by the mind's wishful beliefs or ideologies, can be even more offensive and as destructive than men. These women suffer from what I call "Athena syndrome". Athena, this Greek goddess of war, sprang from the head of Zeus, the supreme Greek male divinity. In his "Eumenides", Aeschylus attributed the following proud statement to Athena: "No mother bore me, in all things my heart turns to the male, save only for wedlock and I incline wholly to the father." Athena was, therefore the daughter of a male, she had no mother, she never achieved maternity or maturity.

Wishful beliefs and ideologies often try to escape from their precariousness and their fear of reality through expansion, through growth, by escaping into a bigger belief or a bigger ideology, by alienating themselves even more from threatening reality. It is in the nature of wishful beliefs or ideologies to escalate towards extremes.

In their extremes, beliefs and ideologies reach a despair in which the most destructive rage takes over. People explain that rage can make us insensitive and blind. Perhaps, it is that insensitivity and blindness, created by extreme beliefs and ideologies that create irritation, despair and rage.

IMPORTANCE

Like any other abstraction, our ego craves to become reality. There is only one way that our wishful self feels a part of reality and that is by becoming important, by being recognized, loved or worshipped, by being applauded or revered or by achieving fame or glory.

Our ego is desperate for importance because of its fragility and fear in its loneliness. In fact it is this fear of loneliness and anonymity that provides the extra energy to try to reach this importance.

In this fear for its existence and survival, our ego leans on our reptilian selfishness, self-centredness, ruthlessness and cold-blooded self-interest, in its strive for territory, dominance or power.

We often dedicate our whole life to the importance of our idealized ego. Most of the time it is our wishful self's importance which dominates our choice of profession, partner in life and the schools and careers of our children.

It is this sense of importance which created and creates a great wastage of energy and resources. The mind's inspired "Homo oeconomicus" rules his economic life instigated more by his ego than by common sense rationality.

The First Class of today's aeroplanes is packed with solemn looking business-men in search of their importance. At least ninety per cent of them could do their business transactions on the telephone, by telex or on a fax machine, but jetting around the world First Class, appeals more to their inflated egos.

Aware of this, airlines have invented VIP's and VIP' lounges at airports, to elicit more travel. Nothing flatters a self important ego better than free caviar and champagne. Funny how a search for importance develops a taste for caviar and champagne. Such is the power of man's mind over his common sense rationality. A great deal of our taste is influenced by our ego's need for flattery.

We go to expensive restaurants because it gives us importance. We buy unnecessary gadgets or luxury goods because they flatter our ego's sense of self-importance.

We spend a vast amount of money in order to visit unknown places around the globe in search of importance.

To call on a sick neighbour or visit an elderly relation, however, does nothing for our self-importance, so is therefore considered uninteresting.

Individual self-adulation and self-importance started expanding in Europe with Greek philosophy. In the VI Century B.C., in his "Golden Maxims", Pythagoras, gave the following advice to man: "Respect yourself most of all." A century later Protagoras stressed that "Man is the measure of all things." I am sure that if Protagoras saw our present ecological disaster, he would have been less sure of his wishful belief. Aristotle pushed Greek arrogant self-infatuation even further when he said: "Nature was right because it has produced a species of slaves, who use their bodies to replace our fatigue"...."It is right and reasonable that Greeks should rule over Barbarians for the latter are slaves by nature and the former are free men."

Man's favourite motto is "know thyself". Most people are aware of this flattering piece of advice of Socrates, because it appeals to their self-centredness. Few people remember that Menander, a leading writer of the Greek "New Comedy", said something far more revealing but less appealing: "The saying "know thyself" is silly. It would be more practical to say: "know other folk".

Few recall A. Gide's important truth as it also lacks appeal to the self-importance mania. "Know thyself is a maxim as pernicious as it is ugly", he said. "Whoever observes himself arrests his own development. A caterpillar who wanted to know itself well could never turn into a butterfly." Perhaps this is why the human species has not yet reached maturity.

Self-importance is a major source of aggression, its definition being "an exaggerated estimate of one's own importance and merit." The aim of any "exaggerated estimate" is to realise itself, which can only be done through aggression at someone else's expense.

Self-importance generates the human passion for dramatisation. In our longing to become "dramatis personae" we create dramas and tragedies. Tragedies have a "certain

31

magnitude", as Aristotle said.

Many people just complicate their lives so as to be able to complain, as complaining gives us an illusion of importance. "Why, since we are always complaining of our ills, are we constantly employed in redoubling them? "asked Voltaire in his "Candide".

Self importance is a great enemy of both communication and relationships. This is unfortunate as self-importance craves communication and relationship, but cannot achieve them because the craving is in order to be recognised and applauded.

Self-importance also breeds boredom.

When , in his "Don Juan", Byron wrote that: "Society is formed of two mighty tribes, the bores and the bored," he was inaccurate. The bores and the bored are one and the same tribe. Concentrated only on themselves, therefore insensitive, the bored are bores.

We consider ourselves superior to nature "Maitres actuel de la planete terre", as Cousteau stressed before starting his campaign against the pollution of the seas.

There is one thing that has always puzzled me. If humans feel so superior, why are they not livelier and happier? Why do they spend their whole lives trying to escape from the reality of nature into illusions and fantasy.

In proportion to body-size, we possess the biggest brain in the animal world. We are proud of this, but a brain that can invent the idea of pride cannot be right. How ironic to be so proud of our big brain. One simple fantasy, one small prejudice, is capable of blocking its entire rationality. One trivial belief can manipulate our brain to the point of blindness.

Self-importance generates the idea of importance. Humans create and cultivate importance in order to be able to integrate into it, therefore increasing their own personal importance.

We glorify humanity merely to boost our self-importance, always identifying ourselves with the object of our admiration.

There are many books illustrating the achievements of our species, but few that mention its failures.

We glorify our national past and we identify ourselves with it to flatter our sense of self-importance. We create celebrities in order to feel important applauding them, following them and meeting them, The applause, however, is usually self-applause.

We build important places in order to gain more self-importance by visiting them.

Many people go to the theatre merely to witness a hit, thereby feeling part of it. Many people attend the opera or ballet just to be seen, to feel important.

Obsession with self-importance encourages the adolescent mentality's excesses and exaggerations, these enemies of natural order, harmony and above all of taste. Excess kills excellence.

In his "Meditations", Marcus Aurelius stressed: "Remember this, that very little is needed to make a happy life." This wise advice sadly only appeals to a minority. The majority of humanity are not looking for a happy life, but an important one.

To creatures from other planets, most human beings would give the impression of a pathetic species running around in circles in search of importance.

Obsessed with its ego's sense of importance our mind invented another absurdity which is the wishful idea of eternity. The mind invented this idea in order to gratify its ego's importance by relating to it. In order to relate better to this idea of eternity, the mind invented another absurdity, the wishful belief in the after life, in life after death.

One of the most negative sides of importance is that the main way to achieve it is by superiority over others. What is more, many people do not try to reach this superiority by improving their qualities but by denigrating, degrading, humiliating, beating or even exterminating or killing others. The idea of superiority created the idea of slaves, aliens or barbarians.

In its insensitivity and blindness a sense of superiority finds its validity in perversion and cruelty.

Many people find the gratification of their sense of

superiority in exploiting others. In fact, the more a person's ego is inflated the more ruthless he is in the exploitation of others.

The mind finds its supreme satisfaction in the exploitation of nature and its resources. By exploiting nature, supernature feels superior to nature.

It is this pleasure of the mind which has contributed in a major way to the problem of the survival of our planet.

The mind's abstract ideas of importance and superiority, which imply inequality, have ruled humanity since the mind imposed itself over the more advanced humane brain. Our political and economic organisations, our military and administrative force, our churches or other institutions, are all ruled on an hierarchical basis.

Hierarchy leans on the reptilian legacy.

The idea of importance created an ugly characteristic; envy.

Envy is often a source of aggression, vindictiveness, vandalism and crime. Envy craves the destruction of the envied. This is best seen in most revolutions which are invariably caused by envy.

The envied often provokes the vindictiveness of envy. Being envied increases an inflated ego's sense of importance. In fact, many display their wealth or power, their decorations or luxury gadgets in order to provoke envy in others.

Envy is destructive because of its hatred, its bitterness and its malevolence. An envying ego is an offended ego.

Envy is debilitating and this reduces the envying person's ability to recover from his envy.

The idea of importance invented the idea of entertainments. We feel important when entertained. Buying a ticket for an entertaining show we are in fact buying a dose of importance for our fragile ego.

Entertainments help us to escape from reality. For an inflated ego reality is intimidating and offending, thus boring.

In this escape into entertainments we lose some of

the efficiency of our senses and perception. In fact, people being entertained are easy prey for pickpockets. In order to render people less perceptive to their economic difficulties or other problems, ever since the ancient emperors, kings or popes up to modern politicians in power, "circenses" or public entertainments or games, were organised.

A sense of self-importance creates vanity and vanity reduces our reasoning. Vain people are easily seduced and manipulated, either by flattery or deceit.

With a sense of self-importance we also develop a fear of death.

The idea of death plays a significant part in our culture and our lives. We are deeply frightened by death. It must have been this deep fear which has been able to reduce our common sense reasoning to the point of inventing or of accepting the absurd belief in life after death. In his excessive sense of self-importance, man has always been desperate to become eternal.

With a better developed humane brain and maturity and with the disappearance of the mind and its inflated ego, this fear of death would also disappear. This would greatly improve the quality of our lives. Fear of death reduces our lives to a sad parody of life.

The ancient Roman Stoics understood that in order to live a life of quality one had to overcome the fear of death. "Qui mori didicit, servire dedicit," Seneca said, meaning that those who do not fear death will never become slaves, that only by liberating oneself of the fear of death can one live life with "dignitas", "pietas", "humanitas"and "magnanimitas", which were the main virtues of the Stoics and which are the main needs or drives of humaneness and maturity. In fact, women who are more mature than men face death with more serenity.

In essence, we are not frightened by death in itself but by our mortality. It is the idea of mortality and oblivion which offends our sense of self-importance.

What is more, with the cult of individualism we acquire another fear. a terrible fear of dying alone. People living in a community are less afraid of death.

Coupled with self-importance, fear of death also contributes a great deal to the mid-life crisis.

The mind's idea of self-importance created another negativeness: greed.

Any gratification of the desire for the importance of an ego increases the ego's infatuation and pretentiousness. This increases that ego's desire for more importance, for more greed. Greed tends to expand.

That greed is our mind's creation can be deduced from the fact that it often develops into mental disorder, into an obsession. In this obsession we never realise that our greed goes against the many needy, or against scarce natural resources, against the future needy.

Consumerism is another consequence of our obsession with importance.

Many people insist that consumerism dehumanises humans. In reality, it is dehumanised humanity, humanity whose humane brain has been silenced by the reptilian legacy, which creates voracity, rapacity or consumerism.

We often buy things not because we need them for our survival but because our fragile ego needs to placate its anxiety. Buying things increases importance. A fragile ego has a sensation of displaying its strength with the act of buying.

The ego's sense of importance, often becomes obsessed with the accumulation of possessions or wealth as, in its eyes, wealth represents power, this supreme aspiration of a wishful self in search of importance.

Obsession with self-importance created another comic aspect of our present day culture: overscheduling.

Overscheduling produces a sense of eagerness, urgency, restlessness or agitation which provides an exciting arousal. This creates rushing.

Being related to fears, rushing carries reptilian selfishness, self-centredness, ruthlessness and insensitivity.

Rushing also reduces the quality of our activities and the quality of the products of our activities, seriously damaging our economy and the quality of life.

It is interesting to notice that the more we increase

our leisure time, the more we rush. This is perhaps because the increase in leisure time increases our sense of self-importance thus increasing our pretensions. In the reptilian existence pretensions follow the reptilian "here and now" gratification which creates a sense of urgency.

In our culture, dominated by the male adolescent mind, sexual relationships are ruled more by the gratification of the male ego's sense of importance than by the preservation of the species.

The present scientific explanation of man's obsession with sex is that his main motivation is to win the reproductive competition and to leave as many of his offspring as possible to transmit and perpetuate his genes.

This thesis cannot, however, explain the fact that men practice safe sex and abortion. This theory cannot explain homosexuality, the sexual abuse of children and other sexual deviations, either.

Man's obsession with sex and with his sexual performance can be deduced from his particular worry about his sexual potency or his virility.

One of the greatest offences for a man's sense of importance was and still is in many areas, his woman's infidelity. In fact until recently women's infidelity was punished with Draconian measures.

CULT OF INDIVIDUALISM

The mind's wishful self and the wishful self's obsession with its self-importance invented the following paradoxical wishful aspirations: the cult of individualism, the cult of individual freedom and the cult of individual sovereignty, independence or autonomy. The Latin word for freedom, "Libertas" originally meant a wishful aspiration or a desire.

These cults are paradoxical because they can only be realised on the expenses of the community, of sociality and togetherness, of loving caring or sharing. In short, these cults can only by realised at the expense of our humane brain, this latest achievement of the evolution of our species.

These cults isolate an individual in his loneliness which increases his fears and in a state of fear there is neither individual freedom nor individual autonomy or independence and even less individual sovereignty. In a state of fear we go back millions of years in evolutionary terms, we go back to the reptilian way of reasoning and behaviour. In this way we wipe out millions of years of the evolution of our central nervous system.

Like most of the mind's wishful aspirations individual freedom and independence tend to realise themselves through expansion or growth. In this escalation they can become mental disorders. In fact, most of our mental disorders are states in which the extreme characteristics of our reptilian legacy come into prominence. These are: cool detachment, indifference, insensitivity, selfishness, self-centredness, violence and here and now gratification.

In its extreme, individual freedom often creates extreme fear, an extreme fear which can produce panic or terror, often total paralysis which is the negation of any freedom.

In its compulsive expansion, individualism can reach narcissism. In fact, we are more and more narcissist species, in which the individual reaches a depressive existence in his self-made individual ghetto, in his solitary confinement.

The narcissist's self-love becomes an obsessive self-absorption in which he develops sterility.

In his self-absorbtion a narcissist only communicates with himself. More and more today's artists apply their empty selves to their work. The purpose of dancing was to create togetherness. On modern dance floors everyone dances with themselves sometimes even in front of a mirror.

A narcissist communicates with himself in order to impress himself. A narcissist tries to impress himself by himself in order to placate his depressing loneliness caused by his excessive individual autonomy. He tries to impress himself because he has failed to impress others. He failed to impress others because they, like him, are insensitive narcissists.

That a narcissist suffers for not having been able to impress others can be seen by his adolescent vindictiveness consisting of his aggressive indifference. With his capricious absenteeism, a narcissist strives to be noticed by his absence.

A narcissist reaches the apotheosis of his aggressive indifference in his active nihilism in which his individual liberty becomes a libertinage, a licentiousness, a nasty game played by sterility.

In narcissism, with its expansion, individual self-interest becomes self-destruction. A narcissist develops what Seneca called "libido morrienti", a death wish.

In fact, much environmental destruction and pollution is due to the increase in narcissism and in its death wish. Those in a suicidal mood tend to contribute to the ugliness of life and the planet in order not to regret leaving the world which the narcissist was unable to change in order to fit his inflated ego. This cynicism should not be surprising as the narcissist is a sterile being and sterility despises the idea of a future. Sterility has no heirs.

One could ask, how is it possible that most of humanity worship cults of individualism, individual freedom and individual autonomy? How is it possible that humanity, which has reached the most advanced stage in the evolution of the central nervous system with the humane brain, opted to retrograde to a life dominated by the reptilian legacy?

How is it possible that humanity is reluctant, in spite of continuous complaining, to abandon this comic and pathetic life dominated by the reptile mentality for a more humane life dominated by maturity and wisdom?

There is only one answer to these questions: our cults of individualism, individual freedom and individual autonomy are our narcotic drugs, our addiction. We are freedom addicts.

Why?

Because, carrying fears or anxieties, individual freedom creates nervous tensions, arousals, which we consider excitements.

What is more, carrying fears or anxieties, individual freedom and individual autonomy help our brain to release its natural opiates, a kind of our brain's morphine, which helps us to become insensitive to the external world, which helps us to escape reality with its order and obligations, which intimidates or offends our mind's infatuation or pretensions. Carrying strong fears, high levels of individual freedom can produce panic, ecstasy, or euphoria.

In this addiction the human mind can produce absurd wishful beliefs. One of these beliefs is the strong belief that we have " an instinct for freedom".

This is an absurdity because in nature ruled by the laws of nature there is no such thing as individual freedom or individual autonomy.

If our individual liberty was an instinct then it would have its natural limits, it would never escalate into libertinage, licence, perversion, cruelty or self-rightousness. Instincts in nature have their innate controlling mechanisms which prevent any excess.

If there was an instinct for freedom, then desire for individual freedom would have been more uniform in space and time. If there was such a thing as an instinct for freedom in nature, then a cell would have never formed a multicellular organism.

People ruled by maturity and by the humane brain's needs, never dream of individual freedom. A caring mother or a loving partner are never free.

We are obsessed with importance and we will sell or abandon our so called "instinct for freedom" for a compliment or a flattery, for fame or money.

We live in a world dominated by the culture of beliefs. If we had "an instinct for freedom" we would never have created beliefs. A believer is never free. That a believer is a slave of his belief can be seen in fanatical believers.

Freedom is related to liberation; liberation is related to a liberator; each freedom has its liberator and each free person or people are slaves of his or their liberator.

In reality liberators liberate people in order to have slaves. The Jewish God liberated His people in order to enslave them with drastic commandments. A liberator ends in becoming a dictator.

Our mind liberated us from the needs of our humane brain, but we became slaves of its beliefs.

In its freedom-addiction, our mind invented an important supplier of its drugs: the Charter of Human Rights which is supposed to guarantee individual liberty.

I feel sure that anyone who proposed to cure stressful freedom addiction with a "Charter of Humane Obligations" would be hated. An addict to any drug hates any cure or anyone who tries to bring him out of his intoxication. That is why any advice to intoxicated humanity to try and achieve maturity can only be irritating and despised. One day, however, the increasing cost of medical drugs and alcohol we consume in relation to our liberty-addiction might bring us to maturity.

We are proud of being capable of "rational deliberations" or "rational judgements".

We do not realise, however, that our rationality is more a reptilian brain's rationality than that of the mature brain's.

The world of the mind is a world of wishful beliefs. The world of beliefs is a world of uncertainty and precariousness, of anxieties and fears. This places our reasoning and our rationality under the influence of our reptilian legacy. This legacy can explain our dialectic, either/or, black/white, violent way of reasoning and deliberating. This legacy can explain our culture of yes or no absolutes.

Influenced, by their reptilian brain, German Nazis

considered the elimination of Jews and Slavs as rational. Their wishful belief in racial superiority brought fear which brought into prominence the either/or radical and violent reasoning and behaviour.

It is also necessary to stress that the reptilian here and now mentality is the mentality of instant involvement. Instant involvement prevents a wider reasoning and a deeper rationality. What is more, once engaged in an instant behaviour, we place perseverance, another reptilian characteristic, into our behaviour which can be highly damaging. In fact, a great deal of our environmental disaster is due to the perseverance of our instant, superficial and often futile involvements.

Our mind is also proud of another wishful belief: "free will" or "free choice".

In order to exercise free will or execute free choice, extra energy is needed. This is mainly created by an added anxiety or fear, as these are which provide the biochemical activity in our body to create the extra energy.

Basically free choice is flight from the alternative, an escape from an "or". It is an "either" which escapes an "or". In fact, it is the fear of the alternative which provides the necessary energy to choose the opposite of the alternative.

We do not exercise our free will or practice our free choice when in a democracy we vote for a political party in an election. We vote for a political party because of fear that the other party might come to power. In fact, it is this fear which provides the energy for going to vote. Indifference towards the political parties creates a political indolence.

Even in suicide we have no freedom of choice. It is caused and provided with the necessary energy, by an excessive fear of life.

The self-emarginated individuals replaced the community with the State. The difference is that while the former is protective because its members belong to it, the latter belongs to its members and is exploited by them. A State is made by its citizens, full of rights and Charters of Rights against it. A community, instead, is built by its members' contributions. Those with the cult of individualism and individual freedom and autonomy consider any personal sacrifice or contribution to society as degrading or offensive to their egos and their importance.

Due to an expansion of the cult of individualism and of the individuals' pretensions this State is in a crisis, disintegrating more and more. The State is less and less able to gratify the increasing expectations and pretensions of its greedy citizens. In order to be able to gratify these pretensions the State invented public borrowing which sooner or later will bring the State to bankruptcy. Citizens seldom protest against public borrowing. Living on credit flatters inflated egos.

In order to be elected, politicians have to increase their promises which can only be materialized by more public borrowing.

What is more, public borrowing reduces the economic possibility to maintain the electoral promises made during election campaigns and this depresses the electorate which in turn damages economic efficiency.

Public sector borrowing damages the economy by increasing the cost of money. Higher interest rates reduce private investments into the productive sectors of the economy, the sector which creates economic wealth.

It is not surprising that a State, particularly liberal democratic States are in a crisis. The State is supposed to help its citizens to fulfil the expectations of their wishful selves. Being an individual's wishful self above the merits of an individual's real self, the State cannot gratify its citizens expectations except by public borrowing, which goes against future generations and of the future of the State.

Bernard Russell explained that liberty is " the absence of obstacles in the realisation of our desires". The State's supreme duty is to create " the absence of obstacles" to the realisation of an individual's desires. As I said, always being above the real self's merits, the wishful self's desires can only be realized at the expense of others, of future generations and the future of the State itself.

Those who succeed in realising their desires are those who are the most ruthless and inhumane. Next to these successful few we have the masses, discontented and offended.

Those successful ruthless individuals created another wishful idea, that of paternal power, based on the wishful idea of the father figure. This paternal power was supposed to replace the natural order of our species organized around the mother and her maturity and humaneness.

Being an abstract wishful aspiration, paternal power implies aggression, violence and brutality. These are provided with the energy created by the fears that wishful pretensions carry with them. In fact, we fear paternal power because it thrives on fear which is a source of aggression, violence and brutality.

Each mind-made power has its own wishful God or divinity which entitles it to the divine rights which create power's self-rightousness. This self-rightousness is often contrary to natural justice or equity.

God, divinities or the sacred, all invented by power, help it to spread fear among the masses. Fear returns people to the reptilian existence in which they accept inequality, injustice, or unfairness more easily.

Paternal power imposed itself with aggression and brute force over maternal order. The difference is, while the former is based on obedience, the latter is based on imitation, or example. A father is flattered when obeyed, a mother feels safer when imitated. A father is "I" indoctrinated, a mother is "we" oriented. A father uses Draconian sanctions and physical punishment against disobedience, while a mother bases her order on the shame of those who oppose it.

Each paternal power creates its own code of justice, its own morality, its own right and wrong. Wrong is punished severely because in the order based on a belief, wrong is considered a sin. The greatest sin in a paternal order is to believe in another god. In order to prevent the masses from inventing another god or another ideology, paternal power tries to limit the mind's activity of the masses.

The supreme aim of paternal order is the father-infant relationship. The Church-faithful and ideology believer relationships are built on this idea. In fact, punishment in paternal order aims at reducing the disobedient rebel to obedient infancy.

The Christian religion shows us a perfect example of this . "Father" priest subjugated the "Mother" Church and the congregation, Her infantile believers. A believer returns to infancy because the fear and precariousness that a belief carries, reduce him or her to be influenced by the reptilian brain, so prominent in infancy.

Man replaced woman in the organisation of our main social unit, the family.

People complain that this main social unit is in more and more of a crisis, lately. Could it not be, however, that the father dominated family has always been in a crisis?

The father dominated family must have been in a crisis ever since it was started because it is against nature. The "Pater familias" is a wishful role invented by man and imposed by his culture. A role has to be performed and a performance carries stage fright, thereby creating a stressful atmosphere in the family. This stress often erupts into domestic violence and abuse of the woman and children. This domestic violence is increasing as man realises more and more that the family does not need a father-figure created by the male dominated culture. Following his adolescent wishful thinking, man idealised the father dominated family. In reality and in nature, a family is organised around the mother, or around a mature, thus maternal father , a father guided by his caring, nurturing and loving humane brain.

Paternal organization is based on hierarchical order, an idea inspired by the reptilian legacy.

This hierarchical order transforms human communications into a parody. The aim of communications is to establish a communion, a togetherness, an intimacy and a horizontal integration.

Hierarchical communications are vertical by nature. Communications towards the superior are servile, aiming at pleasing the superior and this does not create a communion or an understanding. Communications towards the inferior are orders or commandments and these are the negation of any communion or any understanding and even less so of equality or horizontal integration.

Many people might stress that rank and hierarchy exists even among primates and other mammals. But, we have evolved the humane brain because we feared the reptilian legacy of rank and hierarchy. I would like to stress that hierarchy in mammals and in primates is also a reptilian legacy which comes into prominence mainly in fearful situations or threatening circumstances. Eliminating our fragile ego, our mature brain is able, however, to eliminate a great deal of these fearful situations or threatening circumstances.

The best illustration of paternal ideology can be seen in communism.

At the top of a State hierarchical ladder there is always an omnipotent and omnipresent father. Stalin was tenderly called "Uncle Joseph". Tito of Yugoslavia was called even more tenderly "Grand-Papa." Leaders of the Roman Catholic Church, the most hierarchical of churches, are devoutly called fathers.

The supreme aim of paternal authority in a Communist State is to run people's lives from the cradle to the grave. In exchange, paternal authority expects strict obedience from the people at all times. Stringent obedience creates an infant mentality.

It is in this infant mentality, in which the reptilian legacy is highly prominent, that we find the real cause of the fall of the communism.

Communism has fallen mainly because of its economy. The infant mentality cannot provide an efficient economy. An individual with an infant mentality is excessively selfish and strongly self-centred. His reptilian here and now exploitation and his instant opportunism are a serious obstacle to any individual or State's economic planning or strategy, to any rational organization of future economic production and productivity. In fact, no communist government succeeded in realising its economic plans.

The infant mentality does not know what punctuality or order, discipline or personal responsibility, precision or tidiness, all essential for an efficient economy, means.

Living for the here and now gratifications, thus

ignoring the future, the infant mentality is not a saving mentality. Without saving the economy is poorly renewed or innovated. What is more, lack of the notion or care for the future creates an "après moi" catastrophe.

An individual with an infant mentality finds any work a boring activity. He has to be forced to work. Forced labour is not only economically unproductive, but also a serious source of accidents to the working people and to the production.

What is more, for an infant mentality industrial tools are toys which after the initial amusement or excitement are soon broken or neglected. In fact, any communist economy faces an enormous cost for broken or neglected working tools, instruments or machinery.

The infant mentality's negligence causes a great deal of wastage in human and natural resources.

The infant mentality considers the property of the State as " res nullius", or things belonging to those who first grab them. Taking goods from factories or offices is considered the most normal thing to do. It is also considered normal to use the office telephone or car for personal use. There is no notion of crime, shame or guilt in the infant mentality. For this mentality, corruption is considered the most innocent exchange of goods or services.

The fathers of communism never imagined that their well-meant wishful ideology would have resulted in the most inhumane dictatorship. They never took into consideration that a father/infant relationship creates the infant's obedience, which creates an infant mentality. An infant mentality needs discipline and discipline has to be enforced. Enforcement frightens the infant mentality and fear brings an infant even nearer to his reptilian legacy. This creates an obtuse or autistic mentality which needs even more enforced discipline, even stricter State control and an even more ruthless autocracy.

CAPITALISM

Liberal capitalism is an ideology invented by the mind in order to suit the needs of the male adolescent reptilian mentality.

The following are the main characteristics of liberal capitalism: a cult of individualism, a cult of individual freedom, a cult of individual autonomy, excessive selfishness, self-interest and self-centredness, insensitivity and ruthlessness, cruel opportunism, a here and now reasoning and gratification, rapacity and assertiveness, a desire to impress in order to intimidate, individual unscrupulous and callous competition, rivalry, aggression and violence.

These characteristics of liberal capitalism reflect the main characteristics of our reptilian brain which comes into prominence with the increase of our fears due to our escape into the wishful beliefs or ideologies of the mind, particularly due to our obsession with the cults of individualism, individual freedom and of individual independence or autonomy.

Liberal capitalism's reptilian origin can be best seen in its predatory nature.

A good picture of the reptilian origin of liberal capitalism can be seen in any of the world's stock-markets when fear reaches panic in which the reptilian characteristics, behaviour and gestures are so evident. Looking at successful international businessmen in various V.I.P. lounges, one has the impression that these initials stand for the first three letters of the vicious, cold-blooded and ruthless reptile, the viper.

Many people, particularly since the fall of communism, consider that liberal capitalism is the supreme achievement of our species. In reality, liberal capitalism is the supreme achievement of our reptilian legacy.

Believers in liberal capitalism insist that its main characteristics such as selfishness, ruthlessness, self-interest, competition and unscrupulous exploitation of human and natural resources are in human nature, that they are instinctive, our innate drives.

This is absolutely true, but only where male humanity in its adolescent reptilian phase of existence is concerned. It does not apply, however, to humans in their maturity.

Many capitalists stress that liberal capitalism introduces rationality into the economy. Liberal capitalism's rationality is of a reptilian nature, it is a here and now rationality based on short-term profit, which, in the long run, creates environmental pollution resulting in ecological crisis. Liberal capitalism's rationality does not operate on the long term, it does not care about the future.

A mature rationality in economy would try to reduce future instability to minimal proportions. In fact, in capitalistic terms, one could say that the activities of a mature humane brain are a positive investment for a better future.

In order to survive, liberal capitalism has invented consumerism, which consists of unnecessary consumption, a wastage of limited resources, which is very irrational as far as our future life, or life on our planet is concerned.

In tune with its here and now reasoning and instant gratification, liberal capitalism favours economy and life on credit, far from being rational in the mature sense. In its short term rationality, liberal capitalism invented credit cards, the so called plastic revolution, which ruined and will continue to ruin future generations.

One can doubt in liberal capitalism's rationality in view of the many cases of obsession with solving errors of the past or present in industry, by expanding investments. Expanding investments is really more related to a sense of importance rather than to economic rationality.

Liberal capitalism's rationality is seriously reduced by its hierarchical structure. Desperate to please the superior, the information passed by those inferior can be far removed from reality by the time it reaches the top, the actual decision making level.

Liberal capitalism believes in Adam Smith's wishful belief that individual selfishness and self-interest are in the public's interest.

If this was the case then we would not have so many

people in the rich capitalist world living in poverty or below the poverty line (34 million in the USA, 50 million in the European Community). If this was true we would not have the North/South divided. If this was true then we would not have, in most capitalist countries, some kind of State, social or economic welfare or assistance for the many victims of individual selfishness and self-interest.

Adam Smith's "invisible hand", meaning that individual self-interest is in the public interest, does not work, it is not a friendly hand. It cannot work because the self interest of an individual obsessed with his cult of individualism, is not in the interest of his real self, a self ruled by his humane brain towards the interest of the community, but by the interest of his wishful self and its pretensions, which can only be realized on the expenses of others' interests. What is more, any gratification in the interest of an inflated self increases its pretensions, thus its aggression and violation of others' interests. In the USA, where individual self-interest rules supreme, there are miles of ugly public squalor.

Individual self-interest is not in the public interest because it is not in the interest of the economy itself. Economy implies a harmonious coexistence with nature and the environment, which means the minimal effort or stress. More than often our individual self-interest is not based on our individual economic self-interest but on the interest of our inflated ego. Our inflated ego's main aspiration is its importance, its recognition. In order to prove itself, our inflated ego tries to dominate nature, to change it in accordance with its pretensions. This can only destroy the conditions of future economic potential.

Being a wishful belief, the cult of individualism tends to expand, thus expanding loneliness, anxieties and fears and these expand the individual's selfishness and self interest. Since the times of Adam Smith there have been two centuries of steady expansion of individual's self interest which by now has reached its main activity: ruthless exploitation of the State and of public interest.

Adam Smith preceded Darwin and Social Darwinism in which the more ruthless an individual is, in pursuit of his selfishness and his self interest, the better chance he has to reproduce, to transmit his genes to the next generations.

In fact, in order to avoid this reptilian Social Darwinism our species developed the humane brain. Going back to the reptilian mentality we pay in a farcical way. The most successful in our Darwinian competition and selection is also the most stressed which means the least reproductive. The Western world is already reaching a stasis in population growth. A recent research in Denmark discovered that sperm count and sperm efficiency are significantly reduced in the most selectively successful men.

Many insist that liberal capitalism is more economically efficient than any other system.This is not true. Liberal capitalism is more active than any other system but this over-activity is far from being rational or efficient from the point of view of common sense. Over-activity can create wastage and pollution which makes it irrational. In fact, much liberal capitalism's production is unnecessary, superfluous or a luxury.

The origin of liberal capitalism's extra-activity lies in the restlessness and agitation that the precariousness of the individual's lonely existence carries with itself. Fears and anxieties created by the precarious existence of the free and independent individual creates an extra nervous energy craving to be discharged. It is this extra nervous energy which provides liberal capitalism with its economic over-activity. This nervous arousal created by the extra nervous energy reduces the efficiency of our reasoning and rationality. This is best detected in certain important liberal capitalism's characteristics such as: audacity, risk-taking, adventurousness, speculation and gambling.

Inventing the relationship between the ego's sense of importance and a surplus in the production of economic goods, the mind brought a new irrationality into economy. The cult of the individual ego's importance created an economy more oriented towards the gratification of the ego's needs than towards the need for survival and the needs of the environment.

Many people started accumulating economic surplus in order to create wealth and through wealth the supreme aim of self-importance, power. With power man hoped to reach total autonomy or independence.

51

Obsessed by his pursuit of wealth and power, man seldom realises that the more he accumulates wealth and power the more he develops a fear of losing them. Extreme wealth and power can create fears of paranoiac proportions. These fears push man in search of more wealth and more power. Man's supreme ambition to reach his individual autonomy or independence through wealth and power is rarely reached. The price that man pays for this futile pursuit is his susceptibility to various stress related diseases or mental disorders.

Economic growth increases instability. It increases instability because it inhibits adaptation and adjustment, these main aspirations of the living world. The ego's inspired economic growth increases instability even more because it increases the ego's pretensions, the ego's craving for more.

Having created its inflated ego, the human mind cannot invent any theory in economics able to reduce our discontent. The mind's theories have to be made around its ego. Any gratification of the mind's wishful ego increases this ego's pretensions and expectations.

We have been indoctrinated that the surplus of wealth has allowed the development of progress. We do not know, however, what progress really means, but we are proud of it. We are so proud of our progress that we do not realise that with progress, ecological crisis, crime and violence, the use of alcohol and other intoxications, envy, suicide and stress also progress. We are so obsessed with our so-called progress that we seldom realise that this progress has brought what we could call progress related diseases and mental disorders. There is a steady increase in diseases caused by stress or progress related immunodeficiency. The over all cost in real terms, in preventing and curing mental and physical diseases or disorders over the last 200 years, have progressively increased in the industrialised countries of the world. Soon, in fact, we may reach the moment when we will have to spend more on medical treatment and other drugs than we are able to earn.

Many people might say that economic growth and

progress have allowed humanity to conquer space. The Americans are proud to have walked on the moon, but in many of their cities they fear to walk on the street at night. Russians spend months in space, but the majority cannot afford to go to the next village to visit their relatives.

We are particularly proud of the progress made in prolonging our life span. In reality, this progress has merely created a new species, a highly dependent, highly costly and highly pathetic species. A great deal of the budget deficits of most countries are caused by the welfare and medical care of the elderly.

Man flatters his sense of importance by assuming his manipulation of nature is progress.This progress, on the contrary, is endangering the very life on our planet, more and more.

Like any other growth, the growth in wealth which allows for the growth in progress, will escalate into over-growth, the prelude of the end. Over-growth is a prelude to the end because it destroys the conditions which allow the existence.

Liberal capitalism has brought obsession with economic growth. Like any other obsession, obsession with economic growth is a mental disorder. Like any other mental disorder this obsession brings out our reptilian legacy, such as selfishness, ruthlessness, aggression and violence.

Liberal capitalism's obsession, consisting of the maximization of economic growth, is not in the economic interest of the community or the planet, in the long term. This maximization of economic growth is manipulated by the reptilian brain, the brain operating on the here and now profit basis which usually reduces or destroys any economic potential for the future. A here and now maximization of economic growth is like cutting a fruit tree in order to achieve the most efficient and quickest harvest.

Being an obsession, the maximization of economic growth is stimulated by an irritation or a discontent of our mind's ego. What people with this obsession do not realize is that economic growth can only increase the original irritation or discontent because, flattering the ego, economic growth increases its ambition or pretensions, which increases the irritation and discontent.

Growth in nature is feared because it increases instability. Climbing a high ladder implies an increase in precariousness. The general tendency in nature is to aim at lesser instability, lesser fears or lesser discontent. As our main fears and discontents are related to the mind and its wishful ego, we can reduce the growth by reducing or eliminating our wishful ego, easily done by reaching maturity. The best way to gratify our needs is to eliminate our greed.

Governments are proud when they can announce a 3% or 5% growth in domestic production. They should also announce the annual rise in crime and violence, in alcoholism and drug-addiction, in stress related diseases and mental disorders, in the cost of unemployment in the material and moral sense and in the level of pollution and environmental deterioration. The steady increase in budget deficits and in public borrowing of most countries are clear evidence that the cost of the side effects of economic growth are far higher than its benefices.

With its short term reasoning and its instant fulfilment, our present reptilian mentality is attracted by immediate benefits. Our tragedy is that short term reasoning does not take the long term side effects of these immediate benefits into consideration.

PRIVATE PROPERTY

One of the major components of liberal capitalism is private property. This is often considered as man's divine or sacred right, a natural and inalienable right.

In his "Psyche's task", Sir James Frazer wrote: "The effect of tabooing a thing was to endow it with a supernatural or magical energy that rendered it practically unapproachable to any but the owner."......"without doubt the first mission of taboo was to establish property, the basis of all society."

What Sir James Frazer did not explain is the significant fact that his society was formed by a man after he escaped from a community life into his cult of individualism. Protected by a community, man does not feel the need for private property. Sir James did not explain that man's mind invented the sacred, hoping that it could give him the protection he lost by escaping from the community.

Bringing us to the reptilian existence, the cult of individualism brought the reptilian need of territory. The reptilian fears losing his territory and man's fear of losing his individual private property provided the extra energy to defend it. It was not "tabooing a thing" which endowed it with "a supernatural or magical energy" for the fighting: it was fear of not having a territory or an individual private property and fear of losing them once acquired, that provided the extra energy for acquiring them or defending them.In fact, it is this fear of losing his private property that provides man with a pathological desire and an extra energy to expand it beyond any rational need. A taboo is not endowed with supernatural energy but by energy provided by its fear of being profaned.

Karl Marx was wrong when he stressed that it was liberal capitalism which alienated individuals. It was alienated individuals who created liberal capitalism and its pillar, individual private property. In a community in which an individual is less lonely, he is less interested in individual private property.

Many people insist that private property contributes

55

to a better economic productivity. Carrying restlessness and agitation, fear of losing the private property or the desire of expanding it, create an extra activity which, as I said before, can be economically unproductive.

Being created by the reptilian legacy, individual private property perpetuates this legacy.

PROFIT

Another significant component of liberal capitalism is the cult of profit. With this cult many people's activities or attitudes, most of the time, are profit motivated. Many explain that profit-seeking is innate in our nature. This is, in fact, true but only of those ruled by their reptilian legacy, as the reptilian brain operates on the here and now gain principle. This is not true, however, with those guided by their humane brain. Eliminating ego and its fears, the mature brain provides activities and attitudes such as loving, nurturing or caring which are not profit motivated.

Like any other cult of the mind, profit implies expansion, often resulting in profiteering. The bigger the profit, the bigger it wants to be. Big is important in the fragile world of the mind, big gives an illusion of importance and power. The colossal is an invention of the pretentious mind. The colossal is even beautiful in the eyes of believers.

Profit tends to expand because the more we profit, the more restless and agitated we become, the more we pursue profit. In the end many people develop a mental disorder, the compulsive obsession of seeking profit for profit's sake.

Profit, in reality, is less an economic necessity than a need of our mind's inflated ego and its importance. Profit flatters an inflated ego. In fact, profit of a speculative nature which does not create economic goods but merely pleases the ego's sense of importance, is many people's favourite profit.

Foreign exchange transactions of several hundred billion dollars which take place every day are mainly a here and now profit seeking for profit sake, which pleases the operator's sense of importance.

Proof that the idea of profit is related to the mind's ego is that we consider a profit or a gain whatever flatters our ego's sense of importance, even if it is not an economic benefit or of a material nature.

Basically profit is dishonest as it gratifies our ego

which by its very nature is inflated and pretentious. That is why a profit is an exploitation, a theft. Profit leaves victims behind.

In spite of the evidence that profit creates victims, F.A. Hayek, this great apologist of liberal capitalism, repeatedly insists "that striving for profit benefits the masses."

As the precariousness of the inflated ego brings our reptilian brain into prominence, profit-seeking becomes devious, ruthless, aggressive, violent and rapacious. Robberies, frauds, black-mail or narcotic drugs trade are all profit motivated activities. Commercial and financial deceptions around the world amount to a hundred billion dollars each year.

Those taking advantage of the inferior, making a profit at the expense of the ignorant, invalids, the naive and the mentally retarded, all these for whom our humane brain would feel pity and the need to assist or help, believe they have achieved superiority and importance.

"Concern for profit is what makes possible the more effective use of resources," stress the believers of liberal capitalism. The maximization of profit is an obsession of the mind's ego and being an obsession, it results in mental disorder, which limits wider and deeper rationality.

What is more, profit motivated use of natural resources presupposes that these resources are renewable or unlimited. Being in tune with the reptilian here and now gratification, profit maximization with limited resources damages the future conditions of life on our planet.

We are so obsessed by the idea of profit that even biology, which is supposed to be a serious science, reasons in terms of liberal capitalism and its profit-motif. We are informed by this science that males of all species have to fight ruthlessly in order to be able to invest their genes. In this way they receive dividends in the propagation of their genes. For many people life seems to be like a free market which prices out those who are unsuccessful in profit making. Living in the artificial world of the mind, the successful in profit-making can, as I stressed before, have problems with their sperm count.

It is man's idea of profit and profiteering that inspired his ruthless exploitation of his invention of a patriarchal family. This omnipotent father found and finds great fulfilment in the exploitation of his mother and grandmother, of his wives or concubines and even of his children or grand-children. Liberal capitalism would be far less efficient and profitable economically if the rearing of children, domestic and agricultural activities of women were fairly compensated.

Many people insist that liberal profit-motivated capitalism provided the wealth which enabled medical and pharmaceutical research and industry, thus helping to find cures for many diseases and mental disorders.

I would like to stress that without the strenuous life introduced by profit-motivated liberal capitalism, many of these diseases or disorders would not have occurred. The more people are profit-motivated, the more they become susceptible to stress related diseases or disorders. What is more, with all its wealth, the West still cannot find a cure for many illnesses or mental disorders caused by Western capitalism's obsession with wealth in the first place.

Profit maximization makes both the victor and his victim unhappy.

Victims are unhappy mainly because losing offends their egos and victors are unhappy because any profit develops an unhealthy appetite for more profit. In fact, any increase in profit tends to increase restlessness and agitation, arrogance and aggression. This is logical as any increase in profit-making increases our ego's infatuation and pretensions.

The pursuit of happiness is considered by many people as a fundamental human right. In our profit motivated world this pursuit of happiness ends in unhappiness or depression. In our profit-motivated world the pursuit of happiness ends in the pursuit of profit. This pursuit ends in a rush for profit.

Carrying a nervous arousal, rushing creates excitement which is followed by post excitement depression, despair or unhappiness. The pursuit of happiness is an escape from unhappiness into deeper unhappiness.

Being realised on the expenses of the community and the environment and its limited resources, a profit can only be justified if it has been realised with the intention to be used for the good of the community, to improve the community's working possibilities and conditions, or to improve the environment, thereby creating better conditions of life for future generations.

COMPETITION

Another important pillar of liberal capitalism is free competition.

Apologists of liberal capitalism insist that competition is economically far superior to cooperation.

This is true simply because in a liberal economy, dominated by the cult of individualism and the cult of individual freedom, cooperation is impossible, as it results in ruthless individual exploitation of the cooperative community, of each other. The concept of real cooperation belongs to the mature or humane brain and its reasoning.

Free individual competition only makes sense if our planet's natural resources were abundant and unlimited: a paradox. With limited and unrenewable natural resources, individual free competition carries the fight for survival and this brings out the reptilian rapacity of our ego in us, which implies an irrational wastage of resources. Because of its wastage of resources, the planet cannot afford ruthless competition any longer. Life on our planet can only survive through cooperation and, above all, through sharing the planet's resources with future generations.

Many scientists explain that free competition is in human nature, particularly in the nature of the human male. This is true, but only on the level of the reptilian existence. In fact, free for all competition is an innate drive of the reptilian brain, a brain with many fears. Developing our higher brains and with them a reduction of fears through sociality, cooperation, mutual assistance, memory, learning and the possibility to reason us out of fears, we eliminated many fears which irritate and stimulate the activity of the reptilian brain. By developing the ego's avidity and pretensions, we return to reptilian fears.

We return to these reptilian fears, however, when our mind develops the cult of individualism and the cult of individual freedom and the cult of an individual ego's sense of importance.

That our free competition is of reptilian origin can be seen from the fact that it is selfish, self-centred, ruthless, violent and unpredictable. A human competitor is ready to use any expediency in order to achieve victory. It is not a coincidence that with the Rennaissance's revival of the cult of individualism, Machiavelli's motto that "the end justifies the means" became so popular.

That human free competition is inspired by the ego and its craving for importance can be seen from the fact that most of our competition is dictated by a search for assertion, rank, power, prestige, domination, fame or triumph.

An ego's rivalry and antagonism, an ego's either/or attitude, can escalate even further than those in real reptilians. Our competition's aim is to beat, to annihilate and even to kill the adversary. Our competition can be intensified by hatred or resentment. That is why our human competition can be vicious, brutal or cruel, that is why it is often a fight to the death. We are the only species and only in our reptilian existence, able to practice the humiliation or torture against beaten opponents, or to enjoy the victimization of our victims.

Mammalians, ruled by their limbic brains and our cousin the primates, ruled by their new brains synchronized with their limbic brains, seldom practice competition to kill and even less to torture. They do not consider their adversaries as enemies, even less mortal enemies. Their competition is more a display of strength than the use of it.

The dangerous side of man's competition is that man's ego is not satisfied with one victory: it wants, more victories, more victims. This brings us to the tragic situation in which the success of few is realised on the failure of many.

Creating victims, free competition reduces the quality of life to its lowest level. Carrying the animosity of resilience, victims create a tension aiming at vindictiveness.

Believers in liberal capitalism stress that free for all competition is economically productive.

It is evident that free competition implies antagonism, often hatred among competitors. It is scientifically proved that antagonism or hatred blind us, limiting the efficiency of our senses, of our perception and of our reasoning, particularly long term reasoning, most damaging to future economy. Believers of liberal capitalism stress that free competition forces people to reason and be rational. The reason and rationality triggered off by free competition are of a reptilian character, instant or short term.

We often see free competition in glorious terms, since we have been indoctrinated with romantic interpretations of Olympic Games. In reality the Greek competitive games were inspired and financed by the most ruthless political and financial games and businesses in which gambling, betting, corruption and deceit ruled supreme.

Material profit was the most important incentive to those Greek athletes.

Liberal capitalism explains that the most important function of free competition is to reduce the price of goods and services. Most of the time this is another wishful belief.

Often the competitors in a field form rings or cartels in order to exploit their customers better or to divide the market among them in order to maximize their profits. After all the supreme aim of liberal capitalism is to maximize profits.

Even during the last World War between Great Britain and Germany, the chemical giants of these two countries respected their pre-war cartel agreements in the world markets. Dividing the market among them, individuals, rings or cartels operate in tune with the reptilian territoriality.

What liberal capitalism seldom points out is that with the rings and cartels among the producers of goods and among the providers of services, the quality of the goods and services is reduced, which damages both customers and public interest. The "invisible hand" of private interest which, according to Adam Smith and liberal capitalism, was supposed to work in the public interest, seems to indeed be invisible.

Liberal capitalism insists that free competition establishes an order based on individual talents. This is true, but these talents are of a reptilian nature such as selfishness, ruthlessness, brutality, cold-bloodedness, deviousness and aggression.

This human element forms humanity's elite, which dictates our culture and our values. Liberal capitalism succeeds, in fact, in perpetuating the reptilian culture and values, preventing humanity from reaching maturity.

Free competition contributes a great deal to the mind's suffering. We mainly suffer when we are afraid of being offended in our ego, in its importance and in its expectations.

Creating a tension in our body this mind's suffering is able to cause even physical pain or to aggravate an existing one. A lasting mind suffering can create a chronic pain. A great deal of psychosomatic diseases and immunological disorders are either caused or aggravated by the mind's sufferings.

The world dominated by free competition is the world in which fear of failure also dominates. The more our culture glorifies success in competition, the more we dread being a failure. This fear reduces the efficiency of our senses, of our perception and of our reasoning which makes us even more vulnerable and more susceptible to failure. Those who are afraid of falling, for example, are usually the most prone to falls.

Some political ideologies tried to replace competition with cooperation. As I said before, this can only be done if with a new culture we eliminate cults of individualism, individual freedom and individual independence.

Carrying these cults, individuals cannot form a cooperation. With these cults, individuals can only form a cooperative society and this is a contradiction in terms. The term society stems from the Latin "societas", meaning a gang or a group of individuals sharing the same interest. The main interest of the members of a society or a gang is to use the society or the gang for their selfish self-interests. Being pretentious, thus pretending more from the society or the gang than investing in them, an individual's self-interest's aim is to exploit the society or the gang, to realize a profit at the expense of its other members.

A cooperation could only replace individual

competition in a community ruled by maturity, as maturity eliminates the adolescent minded cults of individualism, individual freedom and individual autonomy. Providing safety and protection, thus reducing an individual's fears, a cooperative community enables its members to activate the centres and needs of their humane brains, centres and needs for caring, loving, solidarity, sharing and work, all of which contribute to the community.

The efficiency of the Japanese economy and its productivity, far superior to that of Western capitalism are mainly due to the Japanese sense of community and sense of belonging to the company of which they are employed.

The supreme aim of life is a lesser instability which can only be realized through co-habitation and cooperation. If the organelles of a cell were competing with each other we would never have had the cell, this main unit of life. If the cells did not cooperate with each other, we would never have had a multicellular organism. If the neurons of our central nervous system did not cooperate we would never have a mature reasoning. In fact, when the neurons of our brain are not cooperating or working harmoniously with each other, we develop abstract wishful thinking, we develop the mind with its beliefs, ideologies, myths, fantasies, daydreams, hallucinations,"grandomania", we develop the mania of being superior to nature, our creator and so we create an ecological crisis.

UNEMPLOYMENT

Liberal capitalism and its free competition have created the serious problem of high unemployment of the employable.

Unemployment is mainly created by profit's tendency to expand, to become bigger and bigger. If those in charge of economic production compensated the factors that participated in production fairly, there would be no profit, as the present form of profit would be the community's profit. As I stressed before, profit gratifies an inflated ego. Being above the merits of an individual's real self, an inflated ego's gratification has to be realized on the expenses of the labour force or the environment, or both. It is by exploitation of the workers that profit-making creates unemployment. By squeezing the extra productivity of those employed, profit-obsession reduces the need of employing more people.

The more unemployment increases, the more competition for jobs will appear which will lower the workers salaries. The lower the wage inflation, the lower the cost of production, the lower the cost of production, the better the competitiveness; the better the competitiveness, the higher the profit.

With this reasoning and logic, liberal capitalism has an interest to create and to keep at the highest possible level, the ugly phenomenon of unemployment. Unemployment is ugly because anyone unemployed in free competition considers himself a failure. This implies a feeling of rejection and demoralization, a feeling of being sterile. This is damaging both physically and mentally. In fact, there is positive evidence that long term unemployment brings depression, opportunistic infections or suicide. In this state of depression, the unemployed are reluctant to try to find a new job for fear of rejection. There is a great fallacy in liberal capitalism's wishful belief that the increase in unemployment increases fears in those employed that they may lose their jobs which increases their competitiveness, efficiency and productivity. This is a fallacy because, at a certain level of fears, working people reduce their flexibility, alertness, sensitivity, self-discipline, clear reasoning and above all the joy of living, which reduces their efficiency and their productivity. There is evidence that low unemployment creates higher economic productivity and far less accidents at work.

Many experts foresee a major increase in unemployment during the next millenium, caused by rapid innovations in technology, which will replace working people in economy to twenty percent of the present number.

Those foreseeing this do not foresee the possibility that before long the present form of capitalism might disappear. In fact, one of the factors contributing to the fall of capitalism could be the increase in unemployment. Modern innovations in the technology of production, which reduces the working force,needs an increase in the demand of goods in order to be profitable. This demand cannot but be seriously reduced by unemployment.

In the field of unemployment we find one of the major negativeness of the mind's ideology of liberal capitalism. In order to please the sense of importance of the few successful people obsessed with profit-making, millions have to be reduced to non-existence.

The chronic unemployment of liberal capitalism is also due to the very nature of profit. Being a creation of the here and now mentality, profit seldom becomes a saving which can help plan a long term economy. With our instant mentality, profit is instantly used to make more instant profit.

FREE MARKET

Another basic factor of liberal capitalism is the free market.

Liberal capitalism idealised the free market to such a point as to consider it a mirror of natural order ruled by natural laws. I would like to stress again that each wishful belief or ideology has its own "natural laws" which are always in accordance with its wishful morality or dogmas.

This idealisation of the free market has gone to ridiculous extremes with people like Hayek, who must have written about it in some pleasant chalet in the Austrian Alps in romantic surroundings, when he insists that the free market brings spontaneous order and justice, maximal peace and harmony, the best economic prosperity and that it is in the best public interest. He wrote this in spite of positive evidence of the galloping ecological crisis and the increasing economic misery in the free market world. Had he lived in one of the shanty towns of Mexico City or Calcutta, I am sure he would have been less stubborn in his beliefs.

Being dominated by instant-to-instant decisions, the free capitalist market has no vision, has no consideration about the future, has no long term rationality. All of these contributed and contribute to the world's poverty and the planet's deprivation.

The free market's instant decisions are determined by the atmosphere of panic that the free market creates. This feeling of panic can best be seen in any of the stock-markets of liberal capitalism when the market is shaken by an event or news of a certain political, social or economic importance. In its high precariousness, the free market is easily shaken even by disinformation, lies, fraudulent news or orchestrated publicity or propaganda. Operating in instant terms, the reptilian mentality does not possess the capacity of pondering. With the globalisation of the world's economies the precariousness of the free market is bringing panicky fear to a precipice, which in a global economy reaches catastrophic proportions. In this world, so over-obsessed with speed, instant decisions become even more instant.

The glorifiers of the free market insist that in a state of nature we were totally free. The answer to this is that if we had been happy in the free for all state of nature we would never have developed our humane brain, the brain which developed the need for solidarity and togetherness, sociality and cooperation, sharing and taking care of those who would be eliminated by the free market mentality.

Those successful in free market economy explain that the free market has no morality or moral values, that it is neither just or unjust, humane or inhumane, that it is anonymous and impersonal, that it is natural and objective. This reflects the reptilian mentality exactly, the mentality we acquired by escaping from the humane brain into the mind's world with its cult of individualism and its obsession with individual self-importance.

Those who glorify the free market and free competition always mention those few who were successful, seldom mentioning the masses of victims, the millions of those who scrape a living way below the poverty line. Globally we are becoming poorer and poorer in spite of Western prosperity. What is even more significant, anxieties and fears have increased to dramatic proportions among both the rich and the poor. This has increased and will continue to increase the tension which will finally burst into all manners of revolutions, riots and wars. The cult of liberalism has killed true freedom, freedom from anxieties and fears.

The real picture of free market economy can be seen in the so-called developing countries. These countries have been forced, by the International Monetary Fund, the World Bank and Western Governments, to introduce free market economies. This policy has succeeded in destroying local communities and domestic cooperative economies, creating famine and chaos. With the help of the West these developing countries have been transformed into the underdeveloped countries.

ADVENTUROUSNESS

Liberal capitalism praises risk-taking which is an euphemism for pure adventurousness. Many insist that this adventurousness is in the interest of economic prosperity.

Risk-taking or adventurousness have nothing to do with rational economy as they are activities which are not stimulated by economic reasons but by excitement. Raising our nervous arousal, adventurousness or risk-taking provide excitement.

Risk-taking and adventures imply gambling and speculation which illustrate even more clearly that their origins lie in excitement. All of these activities increase instability and precariousness which inhibits long term rationality in economy. That is why most speculations or gambling end in economic disaster: successful speculations or gambling are exceptions.

Economy is becoming more and more speculative. In this obsession for quick speculative profit, even national currencies, whose function was to facilitate trade, have become speculative or gambling commodities. International speculations on the world's money markets destabilise national economies. Being activities on a short term basis, these currencies speculations inhibit long term planning and investments in national economies. Governments play with the official interest rates, often on the expense of their national economies, in order to protect their national currencies against international speculation or gambling.

Adventurousness implies audacity which means the challenge of rationality and common sense reality. This is carried with arrogance and aggression which increase excitements but decrease the efficiency of reasoning and logic. In fact, a great deal of our present ecological crisis is the result of the Western obsessive pursuit of adventurous excitements over the past five centuries.

There is no adventurousness in nature: it is a creation of the pretentious mind. Adventurousness, in fact, is caused by excessive restlessness, originated by an excessive gap between our real self and its poor potential and the wishful self and its exaggerated aspirations or pretensions.

Liberal capitalism's adventurousness encourages criminal audacity and adventurousness. The more liberal capitalism appreciates risk-taking in economy, the bigger becomes illicit risk-taking, crime and the prison population . The cost needed to fight crime and the cost needed to service prisons is higher than any benefice national economy might get from liberal capitalism's adventurousness in economy. What is more, there are far more unlucky adventures than lucky ones.

WORK

Work is the very essence of life. It consists of an organism's activities aiming at reducing its biochemical irritation or instability to a lesser irritation and instability. The main irritations and instabilities are caused by hunger, thirst, sex and fears.

With our mind's ego and its sense of importance, the nature of work changed radically. Our ego's sense of importance, in fact, is the dominant ruler of our activities. Any activity or work which does not appeal to our ego is considered offensive, degrading, a toil or a sacrifice.

On the other hand we are also the only animals capable of hyperactivity, of being workaholics. This usually happens when the work in question flatters our pretentious ego, when it appeals to the ego's sense of importance.

With the cult of self-importance, our mind created the idea of leisure. Being the opposite of humiliating work, leisure flatters our sense of importance and our cult of individual freedom. Leisure is often the status symbol of an inflated ego.

Paradoxically, however, increasing our sense of importance, leisure is able to increase our expectations, our restlessness, agitation and our rushing. Some people's lives on holiday can be more stressful than their lives at home.

Throughout history we can see that the more the cult of individualism and the cult of the ego's sense of importance are in prominence, the more work is considered a toil, a sacrifice, an effort or a fatigue, a degradation or a humiliation. Ever since Biblical times, work has been related to our downfall.

Work is offending or degrading for an inflated ego because it brings the mind down to reality. Reality deflates an inflated ego. In fact, bringing people down to reality, work can be a good therapy for many mental disorders. Indeed, such disorders are caused by excessive self-aggrandissment, exaggerated self-preciousness or inflated self-infatuation.

With the development of man's ego's sense of

importance regarding work, the practice of service and servants came into being. Aristotle, who contributed a great deal to our present culture, explained that nature was generous as "it has produced a species of beings, slaves, who used their bodies to replace our fatigue."

With the sixth century B.C. , in Greece, man's cult of individual freedom and the cult of his ego's importance started taking place on an important scale.

With these cults, leisure, fantasizing, philosophising, art and poetry became gratifying activities. Leisure was considered the sister of individual freedom.

With the fifth century B.C. Protagoras' motto "man is the measure of everything," started man's egomania and his egocentrism.

In Plato's "Republic" we read: "It is fitting for a man to despise work." Aristotle stressed in his "Politicis" that "wage earnings do not leave the mind either freedom or the chance of elevation."

According to Xenophon, Socrates said: "The workers and their handicraft are discredited and despised in the cities."

It is interesting to note that the despise of work and the denigration of women goes hand in hand throughout the history. The self-infatuated man denigrates woman because he fears her. He fears her because he is afraid that her maturity, which represents reality, might deride his wishful ego.

During what our present culture considers the golden fifth century in Greece, Pericles insisted: "The greatest glory of woman is that her name whether for good or ill, should be as little as possible on the lips of man." Demosthenes stressed: "We have wives for child-bearing, hetairae for companionship and slaves for lust."

The Ancient Greeks illustrated the tragic lives of their women in their tragedies.

A particular fear and hatred of woman was developed by the philosophers. From Plato to Nietzsche, philosophers either ignored woman or were negative about her. The main reproach of philosophers was that woman was unable to be a philosopher. To woman, philosophy was man's philosophising and had no practical value. In fact, philosophy has never provided any usefulness in practical life. On the contrary, it has provided conceit and arrogance and serious political and social damage. Without Plato, humanity would never have had so many disasters caused by Utopian ideologies. Without Hegel and Marx, we might never have had a century of civil war, strife and tension caused by the fight between left and right. Without Nietzsche, we might never have had racial persecutions and holocausts. Being a philosopher, Nietzsche was so far removed from reality as to be able to realise that superman attracts the passions of "underman".

Ever since the sixth century B.C. in India, while the men meditate in search of their inner selves, the women work.

On the other hand, in Ancient Rome, particularly in the first and second centuries A.D., when women were in prominence, work was considered a virtue.

The power of women in Ancient Rome derived mainly from their dominance over "lares" (the cult of the family's dead) and over "penates" (the chief private cult of every Roman household). The Roman "matrona" was also in charge of the most important cult, that of Vesta, the earthgoddess.

The position of women in Roman life is best explained by the famous sentence of Cato the Elder: "All nations rule their wives, we rule all nations, but our wives rule us"...... "Before the Roman matron, nothing could be said which was disgraceful, nothing could be done which was dishonourable," he stressed.

In Ancient Rome, particularly in the period of the Antonine emperors (Trajan, Hadrian, Antoninus Pius and Marcus Aurelius), work was considered a supreme virtue and leisure was considered synonymous of sloth, the source of all vices.

In his "Epistulae Morales", Seneca stressed: "Nihil est quod non expugnet pertinex opera, et intenta ac diligens cure," meaning that there is nothing that cannot be won with persistent work and attentive and diligent care.

In his "Georgics", Virgil, this great poet of nature, explains: "Labor omnia vincit improbus," meaning that with work we can overcome or win everything.

The respect for work in Ancient Rome can be deduced by the motto, stressed by Plautus, in his "Persa", which says: "Age quod agis," meaning whatever you do, do it well.

Dying, Septimus Severus gave his last advise to the people of Rome: "Laboramus," meaning, let's work.

The negative attitude of Christianity towards women and work is well known.

Being based on the cult of individual freedom and the cult of the ego's sense of self-importance, liberal capitalism has to provide incentives pleasing both these two cults in order to induce people to work. Most of our activities and work seem to be related to these two cults.

In our materialistic culture, these incentives have become money and perks.

We often choose our profession in our adolescence when our mental activity is highly influenced by our ego's sense of importance. In fact, few people choose their profession in tune with the economic needs of their future lives, or in accordance with their physical and mental capacities. They opt for careers to please their egos. This makes for stressful lives.

For the inflated mind work is a fatigue or boring, particularly if its remuneration does not appeal to the mind's ego. The higher the ego's pretensions, the higher the ego's aspiration to a higher remuneration of its work. In this aspiration many ambitious people achieve remunerations above their merits, or positions beyond their competence. This is when over-ambitious people develop stress and stress related diseases or mental disorders.

Like any other creation of the mind, pretensions and ambitions tend to expand until they reach their over-growths which lead to breakdowns.

Some politicians advise workers participation in the running of their enterprises as good incentives for work and its productivity. This often creates a curious paradox.

In our present culture, workers participation in running enterprises increases their egos' sense of importance, which increases their pretensions. What is more, any increase in the sense of self-importance decreases the desire to work and increases the desire for leisure. With the increase of an individual's sense of self-importance, fatigue at work sets in.

The participation of workers in running their enterprises is a participation of individuals, each of them carrying his own cult of individualism and the cult of his ego's importance. For these individuals the participation in running their enterprises means a selfish and ruthless personal exploitation of his enterprise. Tending to expand, in the end this exploitation kills the enterprise.

One could ask why, in eras and in communities where there is an appreciation of women, there is also a higher labouriousness and an appreciation of work ?

Women have a better developed humane brain and when and where women are appreciated the humane brain's values and reasoning are more in prominence and work is a strong urge and need of the humane brain.

Activities and work inspired by the humane brain carry pleasure and contentment. Whenever any centre of the humane brain is activated it gives pleasure because it reduces our fears and worries, it reduces our sense of precariousness, our instability and our insecurity. In fact, our humane brain, as I said before, evolved in order to reduce our fears and worries, our precariousness, our instability and our insecurity. Whenever we exercise the humane brain's centre for sociality, friendship or sympathy, we achieve the pleasure of increased security. Any activity or work contributing to the needs of the community increases our sense of belonging which decreases our anxieties. Any time we are caring, nurturing, loving or helping those in need, we feel pleasure.

Those who reason and behave in accordance with their mind's inspired reptilian brains, are often irritated by those reasoning and behaving in tune with their humane brains. That is why men are often irritated by women. That is why when an old-aged pensioner pleads for mercy from a hooligan robbing him or beating him, the hooligan becomes irritated, which merely increases his cruelty and aggression.

The difference between the activity inspired by the

mind's cult of individualism and its ego's importance and the activity inspired by the humane brain, is that the former needs strong incentives which can gratify the ego's sense of importance, while the latter does not need external remuneration or recognition as it carries contentment and pleasure in itself. With the humane brain, work becomes its own reward. Depending on the brain in prominence, work can be either a joy or a pain, a contentment or a suffering, pleasant or repugnant, amusing or boring.

As I mentioned before, exercising one of the centres of the humane brain triggers off the activities of other centres of the same brain. A caring mother is ready to take care of other children, the elderly or disabled, animals and plants, her habitat and the environment. She is able to love her domestic activities and to prevent the wastage of natural resources. She is able also to visualise the future and to take care of the future of our planet. People taking care of a pet are positively more humane than those shooting animals in sporting activities. People taking care of someone in need are less stressed in the office or factory.

Another difference between activities inspired by the mind and those inspired by the humane brain is that the former brings fatigue quicker, while the latter, even when fatigue is reached it is a pleasurable and healthy sensation.

Eliminating mind inspired activities, activities inspired by the humane brain eliminate stress and stress related diseases and mental disorders.

Activities inspired by the humane brain cause far less accidents than activities inspired by the mind. This is because when the humane brain is in prominence our senses and perception, our curiosity and alertness, our observation and reasoning are wider, deeper and more realistic than those which take place when we are under the dominance of our mind. In fact, a fanatic belief or prejudice can render us insensible or blind.

In order to cope with the increasing cost of the old and invalid population better, those able to work must work harder. Material incentives needed to improve the quality and the quantity of the work of the working population are less and less available. The only solution for the future is a better development of our humane brain which carries a need and urge to work. Maturity is fruitful and giving. With the steady increase in pretensions and expectations in our present culture based on individual selfishness, the tension between the working population and the welfare dependents could easily erupt into serious antagonism.

The organization of activities and work by those guided by the mind and the organization of those guided by the humane brain are totally different. The former is an abstract idea which has to force reality to adapt itself to the mind's idea of organization, while the latter is an innate part of the humane brain's activity, an activity in harmony with nature and its laws, an activity of adjustment and consolidation.

In a culture based on the humane brain's values, shame would play an important role. It would be shameful, for example, to receive social security or any welfare from the State without giving back some contribution to the community or to the improvement of the environment. We should not forget that work is the best therapy against old-age decrepitness, against depression and loneliness. Work is also a help in reaching joyfulness, a sense of humour, loving and caring.

A sense of gratitude for receiving help from the community or the State, could significantly reduce the exploitation of the community's generosity.

The world of the mind is a world of wishful beliefs, pretentious ideologies and capricious or excessive desires. This can easily create a sense of guilt.

A sense of guilt can generate apathy or resignation which can affect both the quality and quantity of our work and activities, thereby damaging the welfare of the community.

Contrary to the mind's sense of guilt, which is devitalizing, maturity's sense of shame is invigorating as it carries the need and the energy to repair the cause of the shame, to grow out of it. Could it not be that the German economic miracle following the Second World War was mainly due to a German sense of shame for the atrocities they committed ?

The most significant partisans of liberal capitalism are the middle-classes.

With the growth of cities and therefore urban life, which led to an increase of the middle-classes, the cult of individualism and the glorification of individual freedom rose progressively. Urban culture and style of life were formed and perpetuated by the middle classes. These classes were formed by rootless, errant, lonely, alienated or self-emarginated adolescent mentality individuals. These lonely individuals gave the main characteristics to the middle-classes all over the world. These characteristics were and are: excessive selfishness and self-interest, restlessness and agitation, self-assertion, aggression and craftiness based on unscrupulous exploitation and profiteering.

The middle-class replaced a natural inclination towards openness, sociality and togetherness, with cool privacy and intimidating secrecy.

The growth of the cities with their anonymous way of life, increased individual loneliness and isolation.

The rise of the middle-classes in Northern Europe produced Protestantism, a direct contact between the individual and his God. The Protestant middle-classes separated from Rome more because of the Catholic Church's Canon Law restrictions on the exorbitant interest rates on loans and excessive profit making, than because of faith.

In the seventeenth century the middle-classes found significant support in Cartesian rationalism. René Descartes gave a philosophical platform to the cult of individualism and individual independence. He called the independent individualism's selfish, self-centred, instant or short-term ruthless expediency, reason and rationality.

Descartes' rationality is a product of the reptilian iron logic and reasoning, the logic and reasoning of a self-alienated autonomous mind far removed from humaneness and the community.

Descartes' "I think, therefore I am," should be read: "I think wishfully, therefore I am my idealised and pretentious self." Descartes' "I" is an anti-communal and anti-social inflated ego, isolated in the fantasy and the splendour of its narcissism.

In spite of Copernicus' revolution, which preceded him, Descartes placed the centre of the Universe back into man's self-centred mind.

The cult of individualism reached its glorious period in the Western World in the eighteenth century. During this period, known as "Enlightenment", the self-alienated individual's characteristics, such as unscrupulousness, selfishness, self-centredness and ruthless self-interest,became the individual's "natural laws". These natural laws were a part of the "immutable laws of the Universe". What is more, an individual's selfishness and self-interest were proclaimed to be in the public interest.

In their excitement, generated by the precariousness caused by their pretensions, leaders of the Enlightenment saw the future as a "general progress of mankind towards perfection".

Leaders of the Enlightenment might, perhaps, have been less euphoric about the progress of mankind if they could have foreseen the continuous increase in environmental deterioration, crime and violence, anxiety and stress, stress related diseases and mental disorders.

In their excitement, French revolutionary leaders produced the "Declaration of the Rights of Man." This declaration, in essence, became a guide helping the individual to reach higher individualism, higher isolation and deeper loneliness.

The French middle-class invented their great principles of the Revolution: Freedom, Equality, Fraternity.

In their way of reasoning, restricted by the fear of freedom and excitement's arousal, the "citoyens" and "citoyennes" of France did not realize that these principles contradicted each other. Freedom cannot coexist with equality. The cult of individual freedom and free competition create inequality. Equality kills individual freedom. In its hierarchical nature, fraternity negates both individual freedom and equality.

What is more, each individual mind has its own wishful idea of freedom, its own wishful idea of equality and its own wishful idea of fraternity. Perhaps this explains why the middle-classes, particularly the French, are so passionately litigious, or quarrelsome.

The middle-class created its own State: a nation-State, a nationalistic or patriotic State. Being based on wishful prejudice of national superiority, patriotism generates anxiety and anxiety's nervous energy. This nervous energy, restlessness and agitation, contributed a great deal to nationalistic or imperialistic wars.

Establishing itself in the Western World, the middle-class mentality introduced its values into Western culture, philosophy, science, ethics and economics.

The urban middle-class mentality enriched its language. Flowery or euphemistic language became of vital importance in a mentality leaning on roles,poses and assumed wishful selves, a mentality trying to impress. It must have been this mentality of poses and masks which invented and perpetuated the theatre and theatrical verbal dexterity.

Because the brain of the urban middle-class is influenced by its reptilian legacy, is perhaps the reason why its language is colder and more distant than the emotional language, expressions and gesticulations of the humane brain.

Affectation, facades, deceptions, ritualism,formalism or mannerism became the essence of life for the urban middle-classes, a life of urbanity. Urbanity became a virtue or a sign of refinement. Anything that was not urban was vulgar: in other words, anything that was natural was uncivilized. The middle-class mentality considers itself above nature and naturalness.

Language and the other means of communications are essential in nature to create understanding, sociality and community. With our technological and scientific achievements in communications, we have achieved the contrary, we have increased our isolation and loneliness. Perhaps, this is because we are more and more intimidated or frightened by informations and communications as they are inspired and propagated by the culture which is inspired and propagated by middle-class minds, minds capable of treachery, lies, deceptions and disinformation.

The reptilian origin of the middle-class mentality can best be seen in its cult of individual distance and privacy, its fear of intimacy or physical contact. The reptilian origin of the middle-class mentality can also be seen in the middle-class' fierce competition for social status which reflects the reptilian ruthless competition for rank.

In his escape into privacy, the middle-class lonely individual became prudish. Prudery influenced dress fashions and nudity or naturalness were considered indecent or obscene. It is interesting to note that in parts of the world or periods of history in which there was no strong middle-class influence, no such word or concept of prudery existed.

In the nineteenth century, middle-class prudery reached its extreme when it was considered necessary to put skirts on tables and chairs in order to hide the legs!

To the mature mentality, nudity inspires playful intimacy or touching tenderness.

With the rise of the middle-classes the use and passion for mechanical clocks arrived.

What could have inspired the passion for mechanical clocks? What kind of mentality could have started adapting its biological clock to an artificial one?

Only an over-ambitious or pretentious mentality could have disrupted its biological rhythm with a mechanical one more in accordance with the mind's aspirations or desires than with the biological needs of the body.

The gap between the adaptation to the mind's mechanical clock and the body's biological clock creates tension, anxieties, stress and jet-lag.

Discovering time, the middle-class mentality started exploiting it unscrupulously.

The avid exploitation of time created a sense of urgency: time famine. To a precious ego, time is precious. "Time is money," as the saying goes, which of course is true for those who worship money.

Many try to gain time by rushing. Increased rushing has led to queueing and congestion, thus losing time. But, although we are aware of this we still persist. Perhaps it is because the frustration of queueing and congestion increases the stress-induced opiates in our brain. We seem to be more and more addicted to stress.

Many insist that the middle-class and its values are in a crisis. The middle-class and its values were always in a crisis. Middle-class culture and values are those of the mind based on wishful beliefs which are permanently in a critical state of precariousness. This is evident from the restlessness and agitation of the mind dominated world and by the tendency of the mind's beliefs to expand. Expansion or growth, as I stressed before, are caused by instability, irritation or discontent.

What we are seeing now is the last phase of this expansion, the end of the mind's world of wishful beliefs. Expansion of the mind's beliefs is reaching its over-expansion, which is always followed by collapse.

We are reaching a phase of nightmares, the natural end of day-dreams and illusions. We are reaching the horrors of hell, the logical end of wishful beliefs.

I have already explained how the expansion of the exploitation of time ends in rushing. In its expansion the mind's cleverness which helped the West to conquer and to devastate the world, is reaching general corruption. The expansion of individual freedom is heading for over-growth in its chaotic panic. The expansion of individual selfishness is reaching a petrifying loneliness. The expansion of self-centredness is reaching the lonely life of a blind person, blinded by self-conceit, in front of his own wishful reflection in an empty mirror. In their expansion the mind's caprices have reached a state of obsession, of mental disorders. In their expansions even excitements have become stressful: excitement-addiction has become stress-addiction.

But, what is the most humiliating for the mind is the comic fact that in its expansion, liberal capitalism, this very pride of the mind, is reaching the pathetic state of bankruptcy, a sad existence on credit.

Increasing fears, our living on credit magnifies the reptilian inheritance of the here and now gratifications which accelerates consumerism. Killing savings, consumerism has killed any idea of order or the future. Without these two ideas the mind's world has reached an extreme instability which carries suicidal agitation and vindictive destruction.

THE FALL OF CAPITALISM

The fall of communism, this important ideology, could be a sign that we are ending the Second Millenium with the beginnings of serious doubt in the validity of the mind's abstract wishful beliefs or ideologies which have kept humanity under their spell for so long. There are signs that the mind's wishful beliefs and ideologies are losing the battle against reality, which these beliefs and ideologies tried to dominate in order to adapt it to man's self-made image of himself.

Liberal capitalism considers itself a rational and pragmatic system, as did communism for seventy years in Soviet Russia. The communists even called their ideology "scientific socialism." Each ideology considers itself the most rational, the most pragmatic, above all other ideologies. In fact, all ideologies are rational, but only to their believers.

To the mature way of reasoning no ideology can be rational for the simple reason that they are out of reality, the source of natural rationality. It is this reality, like over-population, pollution of the environment, destruction of the planet, which are deriding ideologies more and more.

The irrationality of liberal capitalism often reaches comic proportions such as the European Common Market's agricultural policy. The countries of this market protect themselves against cheap food from poor countries, which keeps up the cost of living, in order to help their farmers produce the superfluous which has to be stored and pay for storage with people's taxes.

The irrationality of communist economy is best illustrated with the following joke which was circulating in Soviet Russia when communism was in power.

It is a conversation between Ivan and Alexis in Moscow.

Ivan: "Have you heard that the Government has started producing supersonic aircraft ?"

Alexis: "How can that help me ?"

Ivan: "Well, if you hear on the media, for example,

that a butcher in Leningrad is selling fresh meat, you can be in Novgorod in few minutes."

Alexis: "Why Novgorod? It is miles from Leningrad."

Ivan: "Because by the time you get there, the queue outside the shop in Leningrad will stretch as far as Novgorod."

In reality the fall of communism means the fall of the capitalism of a State, a State in which liberal capitalism's ruthless mentality was adopted by the communist nomenclature. Individuals of this political oligarchy were guided by the mentality of a cruel exploitation of human and natural resources for personal interest. In fact, after the introduction of free market economy in former communist countries, most members of the communist oligarchies have become millionaires.

Capitalism and communism hated each other to the point of blindness. They hated each other, not so much as two different ideologies but as two reptilian minded competitors fighting for global territoriality, for the dominance of the world.

In order to fight each other more ruthlessly, capitalism and communism depicted each other in the most vitriolic and evil terms. This was done in order to increase fear of the enemy. Increasing fear, increases the reptilian cruelty and aggression, so necessary to eliminate the enemy.

After the fall of communism, of its dangerous and evil competitor, Western capitalism is starting to question its own ideology and its own values, now even questioning the validity of all ideologies.

This reaction is mainly due to the fact that once its competitor is eliminated in the race for world power, the West is emerging from the nervous tension, kept alive by the competition, that was limiting its wider reasoning. With a deeper and wider reasoning the West is starting to question the validity of the race for power, of power itself, of its culture and its values. In this wider and deeper reasoning, the West is beginning to realise the enormous wastage of the planet's finite resources over the last seventy years, mainly caused by its competition with communism.

Our present economic recession in the Western

World is, in reality, a more mature and a more rational approach to economy following the euphoric over-spending and the irrational life of debts, caused by the reptilian here and now gratification mentality, created by reduced reasoning, reduced by the nervous tension kept alive by the fears of the enemy in the ruthless competition between two insensitive competitors.

The most serious factor which is forcing the fall of capitalism is ecology, mainly the preservation of the planet and the life on it.

Liberal capitalism which consists of a free and massive exploitation of natural resources is in fact an ideal system, but only for a planet with unlimited or renewable natural resources. Apologists of liberal capitalism have never taken into consideration that our planet's natural resources are limited or finite.

If the liberal capitalism industry has to pay for the repair of the damages to the environment and if it has to limit the exploitation of natural resources, or if it has to modernize its technology so as to limit the degradation of the living habitat, then liberal capitalism would be costly. The increased cost of goods would limit the demand, limiting the very soul of liberal capitalism: its profit. In order to be able to make a profit in accordance with the ecological needs, liberal capitalism can only reduce its production costs by reducing the labour force, by increasing unemployment. Increasing unemployment reduces the market's demand of goods and services, resulting in wide-spread bankruptcy.

By becoming a decisive factor in future economy, ecology will eliminate liberal capitalism's expansion. Like any other ideology, liberal capitalism has to either expand or fade away. Ideology does not operate with the notions of adaptation, adjustment or consolidation to the conditions imposed by reality or by nature.

The second important factor contributing to the fall of liberal capitalism is the increase in population, which in its expansion has already reached a state of over-population.

If Adam Smith was alive to-day, he might have not written that "the most decisive of the prosperity of any

country is the increase of the number of its inhabitants."
This could only have been valid if the natural resources of
our planet were unlimited and if material prosperity was not
damaging ecology. If Adam Smith had been right, China
would be a hundred thousands times more prosperous than
Luxembourg, for example.

How a wishful ideology can blind even those who
are considered great minds is evident by reading what the
important apologist of liberal capitalism, F.A.Hayek, wrote:
"In any case, there is no danger whatever that, in any
foreseeable future with which we can be concerned, the
population of the world as a whole will outgrow its raw
material resources and every reason to assume that inherent
forces will stop such a process long before that could
happen."...... "The modern idea that population growth
threatens world wide pauperisation is simply a mistake," he
added.

The authoritative Washington-based Worldwatch
Institute stressed that the global grain production rose one
per cent a year between 1984 and 1990, while world
population rose two per cent a year. This is happening when
over half of the world population is already either dying
from starvation, or undernourished or living below the
poverty line. There is evidence also that every year more and
more land is becoming infertile and that fish stocks and
underground water supplies are becoming greatly reduced.

Hayek was a good Christian and a fervent believer in
God's message to men: "multiply and replenish the earth and
subdue it."

When God was supposed to have said this, the
planet was rich in natural resources and the world population
could not have been more than about two hundred million
people: a vast difference if compared with the present world
population of five and a half billion.

When the Judeo-Christian God was emanating His
Commandments or recommendations, there were less people
in need of help and more humaneness ready to help. When
God was talking to His people it would have been a mortal
sin to abandon a sick member of the family. Nowadays
more and more people abandon their parents or elderly
relatives to community care. In the USA "granny-dumping"

is more and more practiced. "Granny-dumping" means abandoning an old, decrepit or disabled relative, mainly those suffering from loss of memory, in front of a hospital or an old people's home, or even in the middle of a square or street. Like many other American practices, "granny-dumping" might soon invade the rest of the world.

When God gave His Commandments life expectancy was approximately forty years. Nowadays it is around seventy. With this expansion, the population of elderly comprises twenty per cent of the total population of most West European countries.

What is more, when God was around there were fewer mentally and physically handicapped people than to-day: 42 million in the USA, 30 million in the European Community. In fact most of the increase in world population is the increase in the passive and community-dependent population. If the organ transplant technic becomes even more efficient, we will soon have an increase in the invalid population.

Lately some American scientists who are obviously more interested in fame than in the welfare of humanity, promised to find the longevity gene in order to prolong human life from two to six hundred years. What these scientists fail to admit is that they will merely be prolonging the age of decrepitness and dependency, not life as such.

It is this welfare dependent population which is another main contributor to the fall of liberal capitalism. It is the increase in this passive and welfare dependent population which is steadily forcing liberal capitalism towards insolvency.

In its growth in number and in the growth of its pretensions, this welfare dependent population has already become a serious burden for the community. Most Western Governments are running vast budget deficits in order to finance this population. Before the First World War , in the USA, only three per cent of the gross domestic product went towards public spending, now it has reached fortyfour per cent. In other countries this increase is even higher.

In most Western capitalist countries the budget deficit is reaching five to ten per cent of the annual national income. Most of these countries can only compensate this deficit partially with a one to four per cent increase in their gross domestic product. The difference has to be borrowed. This public borrowing has already reached astronomic figures, vastly increasing the interest on the borrowed money, which has to be financed by further public borrowing. This is a sure route to bankruptcy.

The road to insolvency is best illustrated by the American economy, the main representative of liberal capitalism.

In 1992 the USA's national debt rose to 4,000 billion dollars. The servicing of this debt for that year cost the Federal Government around 300 billion dollars. Over the last ten years the American national debt has gone up from 36 per cent of the gross domestic product in 1982 to 70 per cent in 1992. There is little hope of reducing this trend without serious political and social disorders.

The American federal budget receipts in 1992 were 1,075 billions against the Government's expenditures of 1,475 billions, which shows an annual budget deficit of 400 billions. Two significant items in the Government's expenditures are the so called entitlements (social security, medicare and medicaid) which represent 52 per cent of the total expenditures and the interest paid for national debt, which represents 22 per cent of total expenditures. These two items cannot but increase. No politician in search of re-election would dare to propose or to vote for a reduction of the indexed entitlements, entitlements which are mainly financed by borrowing further. What is more, the steady increase of the elderly, invalids and of the welfare dependent people, can only increase the amount needed for these entitlements.

On the other hand, massive public borrowing reduces credit availability for private investments. Reduced private investments, which carry an increase in unemployment, reduce the Government's fiscal revenues, which increases budget deficits, thus increasing national debt and the interest needed to service this debt.

By now, in most countries of the world, any new baby is born insolvent. Often for the rest of his or her life the newly born will have to pay interest on the loans made by his or her parents or grandparents.

Liberal democracy, the major ally of liberal capitalism is also a significant contributor to the decline and fall of liberal capitalism.

In order to be elected and in order to preserve its power once elected, liberal democracy's politicians promise to improve the care and assistance of the welfare dependents. This welfare dependent population is more and more a determining factor in political elections. Any fulfilment of these promises increases budget deficit and public borrowing.

In the decline of liberal capitalism lies another farcical game, probably inspired by nostalgia towards the imperial past and glorious profit-making of the colonies.

In order to improve the demand of their industrial goods and services by Third World countries, developed countries borrowed money in order to lend it to the developing countries. Many years of this policy have transformed the traditional economic, social and political lives of these countries into economic misery, social chaos and political corruption. These countries are now in the situation in which they have to export the raw material of their precious natural resources at cheap prices, damaging global ecology and future generations in order to pay the interest on their loans, which have often been redirected to the private accounts of politicians in London, New York or Zurich.

After having spent billions of dollars in Third World countries there are only a few projects mentionable as economically viable. This is most unflattering for the so-called experts of the International Monetary Fund, of the World Bank or for the experts of the developed countries, who were supposed to advise the developing countries on how to use the loans in the first place. Having met many of these experts, I am not surprised that their advise ends in causing starvation in Africa and in Latin America, the rich getting richer and the poor getting poorer.

The rich countries of Group Seven are sending their economic advisers to former communist countries in order to teach their leaders how to run their economies. This is when

Group Seven countries are suffering a serious economic crises themselves, unable to solve their own problem of unemployment, increasing poverty and squalor. One has the impression that the so-called rich countries are behaving like drug-pushers, trying to attract more people to their own drug-addiction. " The more the merrier," seems to be the motto of all tragedies.

Sometimes liberal capitalism's countries finance their domestic demand with a reduction in direct or indirect taxation, In order to compensate the loss of their incomes created by the reduction in taxation, governments are forced to borrow money in order to reduce the budget deficit. Governments are often forced to increase this borrowing in order to pay the deficit in their foreign trade as reduced taxation increases the demand for foreign goods and services.

In order to increase this demand, ruthless liberal capitalism committed one of its most atrocious crimes. It started giving the young, inexperienced and naive, credit cards. Their egos intoxicated by flattery, the young began an euphoric consumption. But, as always, boom is followed by doom. The difference between the two is that the latter lasts longer.

Those trying to find a solution for the crisis of the world economy are of the same mentality and often the same people who created the crisis. They cannot seem to grasp that in a crisis it is the extreme reptilian mentality which comes into prominence, the mentality for instant remedies, remedies in tune with the reptilian mentality's here and now reasoning, which can only aggravate the crisis because it is this instant reasoning which created the crisis in the first place. Crises cannot be solved, they can only be prevented. Prevention of crises can only be done with a reasoning in which the concept of the future plays the main role and this is beyond the capacity of the reptilian brain.

There is another significant factor which contributes to the decline and fall of liberal capitalism.

The more successful liberal capitalism is, the more

material growth it produces, thus increasing people's expectations. With an increase in expectations and pretensions, envy towards those who are more successful increases. Liberal capitalism creates inequality and nothing offends an inflated ego more than those who are better off. In fact, it is not so much the welfare dependent people who insist that the rich should contribute more to their welfare, but the lesser rich, who insist that those above them in wealth should contribute more towards the assistance of the old and those in need. Imposing higher taxation on those who try to create the position of being envied, reduces the validity of liberal capitalism.

Inflation is another major contributor to the decline and the fall of liberal capitalism.

This plague of modern economy is very much a consequence of the chronic increase in the individual's pretensions. Inflation is in tune with our mentality's tendency to be compensated beyond our merits and to consume above our earnings. It is interesting to note that in 1991, the year in which Italy was running records in budget deficit, public borrowing and inflation, Italy was also the highest world consumer of French champagne and Mercedes cars. "La dolce vita" has always meant life above one's means.

Inflation favours speculation which increases instability and uncertainty, both serious obstacles to rational long term planning and a healthy economy. World economy is becoming more speculative than wealth creating. This speculative activity is mainly concentrated on money markets where national currencies are traded twenty-four hours a day. The importance of these operation can be seen by their daily volume of several hundred billion dollars. This volume of operations can ruin any currency and any economy throughout the world in a matter of minutes. There is no national bank or even a group of national banks in the world which have sufficient reserves to fight an onslaught of this volume.

The dramatic consequences for a currency and its economy are caused by the unilaterality of the direction of the international money markets' assault. As I said before, liberal capitalism's markets and particularly foreign exchange markets are in a permanent state of panic. When in a panic individuals tend to transform themselves into a mass, a mass of individuals imitating a leader. It is enough that the Tokyo market or that of Hong-Kong starts to sell Italian Lire or British Pounds, for the rest of the world markets to follow.

Like cold-blooded predators choose the most vulnerable prey in the pack, so the speculators of foreign exchange markets select the weakest currency, in order to assault it "en masse". Once these speculators assault a currency, no-one can save it from devaluation which is how they realise their profits and which encourages them to look for more excitements, for the next easy prey.

Facing a permanent threat from the foreign exchange markets' speculators, most national currencies and economies are in a permanent state of defence, their only defence weapon being the official interest rate, which is in a state of permanent alert. By now, most countries run their economies on a day-to-day , or a short-term basis, ruled by the trembling official interest rate.

Existing in a state of defence against the invisible enemies of the foreign money markets' speculators, most national economies are run with here and now opportunistic expediencies leaving the future to be dealt with when it comes, with another instant expediency which causes positive losses in economy and even more positive uncertainty which increases the reptilian mentality.

Our great mind, which we consider our supreme achievement, has reduced humanity to a pathetic situation: our economic policy, our life, often our survival, hangs on an ephemeral gadget, the domestic or national official interest rate, determined by the speculative caprices of invisible international forces, out of control of national governments. One per cent, often even a half per cent rise or fall in the official interest rate can bring serious consequences to a national economy: such is the precariousness of economic life created by the mind's theorising.

In order to survive, or be re-elected, many

governments pray to God to placate the international invisible forces to allow a reduction in their official interest rates. With cheaper loans governments hope to stimulate demand and the revival of investments in industry, which might reduce unemployment.

With our here and now reasoning and mentality, cheaper loans increase investments in short term speculations much more than in the long term wealth creating industry.

What is more, cheaper loans increase consumerism, reducing savings and increasing inflation. Without savings, precariousness increases and with this our reptilian reasoning and behaviour. Without savings it is more difficult to plan or organise the future rationally. Lack of savings and inflation kill the future in the name of the present.

Economy based on debts and inflation creates high anxiety. In more and more people this anxiety is reaching a level in which it becomes physically and mentally exhausting, creating indifference and apathy which can seriously damage the economy. I have already stressed how a high level of unemployment, threatening even those employed, can reduce the efficiency and the productivity of working people.

Some short-sighted economists and politicians claim that a certain amount of inflation can be beneficiary to the economy. The simple answer to this reasoning is that a little bit of inflation is like being a little bit pregnant: it is liable to grow.

Nobody pleased the selfish, self-centred and short-sighted humanity more than John Maynard Keynes (1883-1946). He advised individuals and governments to spend beyond or above their earnings. He justified the ruinous life of credit with his cynical remark: "In the long run we are all dead."

Perhaps, Keynes did not care about the future because, due to his sexual deviation, he did not have children.

The main cause of the decline and fall of liberal

capitalism was, however, its victory over the communism.

Liberal capitalism did not realise that victory over its adversary would also imply its own end. In order to prosper, an ideology needs an enemy. By conquering the enemy, an ideology drifts into apathy, reducing it to atrophy.

ECOLOGICAL CRISIS

We all complain about the ecological problem and the degradation of our habitat, which could reach serious proportions quite soon.

The United Nations survey on the environment of 1992 forecasts the future in gloomy terms.

The present world population of five and a half billions could easily double in thirty years time. In the meantime the agricultural production and its potential is diminishing. If the growth of the world population is not limited it is bound to expand beyond the capacity of its habitat.

The destruction of the rain forests is contributing to the shortage of drinking water. In fact, many experts forecast that this shortage will cause international tension and fierce struggles for its sources.

The world's fishing catch is close to reaching hundred million tons a year which is considered the limit over which any new catch would undermine replenishment.

Air pollution, particularly in urban areas, is already sinking to health damaging levels.

The thinning ozone layer is expected to increase skin cancers, blindness and opportunistic infections, infections due to a lesser efficiency of the immune system, caused by the increase in ultraviolet radiation.

A United Nations' survey stressed the seriousness of the problem by underlining the rapid disappearance of many species.

What this survey failed to mention is the fact that people's expectations are steadily increasing, which creates disappointment, discontent, gloom and depression, which result in indifference and apathy, all of which aggravates the ecological crisis.

What the U.N. survey did not mention either is that the increasing pollution and ecological degradation create environmental ugliness, which is frightening and dehumanising. In fact, the reason most people find beauty in symmetry and harmony is because these are more calming , they frighten us less.

The U.N. survey also failed to mention that, modern life's noise often increases blood pressure, heart disease, ulcers, asthma, headaches, fatigue and helplessness, Creating anxiety, noise returns us to our reptilian inheritance, increasing our aggressiveness and violence.

Noise also reduces the sensitivity of our auditory mechanism which plays an important part in mental and physical balance. This illness can easily bring our reptilian legacy to the fore. Loud military music and the noise of guns in battle can bring out an extreme reptilian brutality.

The continuous increase in the density of the population of big cities stimulates people's endocrine system of defences, which increases stress and stress related disorders and diseases.

The U.N. survey forgot another important fact. Stress, caused by ecological degradation, seems to be a major cause of the reduction in sperm count and in the quality of semen.

This stress, caused by ecological degradation, also seems to be the main reason for the widespread increase of abnormalities in the genitourinary organs or in man's reproductive system. Clear evidence shows that both these disorders are more pronounced in more polluted areas.

More and more people are involved in environmentalism or in the various ecological movements. In our culture, dominated by beliefs and ideologies, even environmentalism has now become an ideology. Being a wishful abstraction, an ideology tends to expand in its materialisation. Expansion implies aggression and violence and these limit rational reasoning. In its expansion, an ideology often reaches over-expansion. It is then that an ideology kills its own cause. Over-expansion usually ends in an explosion. It is then that an ideology reaches its ridicule.

There are more and more cries of "Life is in danger", "The planet is in peril".

One thing is positive. The ecological crisis is of man's making. Our culture, based on the mind's wishful beliefs and ideologies, pretensions and arrogance, has brought the planet and life on it, to grave danger.

Our mind proudly insists that man is the master of his own destiny. This destiny had ended in an ecological disaster. Slowly but surely we are killing our environment, our creator, our mother earth. But, it is in the nature of the mind's super-nature to kill its creator. It is in the nature of adolescent man to destroy or denigrate his mother. By doing so, he has an illusion of emancipating himself, of achieving masculinity, this abstract wishfulness.

I would like to stress, however, that the ecological crisis is the best thing that could have happened to humanity. Only an ecological crisis could have shaken the arrogance and blindness of human conceit. Only an ecological crisis could have started questioning the validity of our culture which the mind's world considers the one and only culture, valid throughout time and space. This culture leans on Utopian Greek philosophizing, on Judeo-Christian self-rightousness and on Enlightment's conceit.

Only this crisis can help humanity to reach maturity, to replace the mind with the humane brain, to replace the cult of individualism with the spirit of community, to replace unhealthy and ruthless competition with salubrious and economically more productive cooperation.

The ecological crisis will help us to realize that we can only solve this crisis by abandoning the mind's pretension to dominate nature in the name of abstract wishful ideas and instead start to imitate nature, to cooperate with it. This can only be done by abandoning the adolescent mind and its inflated ego, for maturity.

This ecological crisis will help us wake up from the fantasy and fiction of the mind and come out from our world of self-flattery and self-deceptions. This crisis will help us to abandon the unhealthy life of excitements for sensible activities inspired by the needs of the humane brain.

This ecological crisis is the best evidence that life, dominated by the mind, was not in our best interest, nor in the interest of other species on our planet.

This ecological crisis will shake the arrogance carried by the mind's beliefs and the blind stubbornness carried by the mind's ideologies.

This crisis will help us to realize that the pursuit of our ego's success emarginates us, isolating us in a depressing loneliness.

This crisis will rehabilitate woman, as she will realize that it is mainly due to the desperate desire of man to prove his wishful image of himself.

This crisis will help us to realize that most of humanity spend their lives in pursuit of unnecessary gadgets. We could soon become aware that these unnecessary gadgets which flatter our egos are our masters as they rule our metabolism, our speed, our greed, our consumerism, our anxieties and our fears.

This crisis has already started questioning the validity of the cults of individualism, of individual freedom and of individual autonomy. Above all, this crisis has started questioning the validity of liberal capitalism and free-market economy.

This ecological crisis might soon start questioning the seriousness of Judeo-Christianity. After all, it was the Judeo-Christian God who ordered men to subdue nature. We are learning to realise that subduing nature means degrading it or destroying it. Entitling men to rule, to dominate, to rape and to ruthlessly exploit nature, God has proved that He is not omniscient: He obviously did not know that our planet's natural resources were limited.

The Judeo-Christian God and his followers created in His image degrade and rape nature because they fear it. They are frightened that the reality of nature might deride their super-nature.

Man believes he is superior to nature, that he is the centre and purpose of the universe. This belief is so strong as to reduce the efficiency of man's senses, perception and reasoning to the point of being unable to realize that the side effects of his belief in his superiority over nature is damaging his habitat and the biosphere. Nature created man and what nature creates, nature can also eliminate.

Our mind considers our species as a supreme achievement of evolution. In this case something must be wrong either with our mind or with evolution as we are mentally and physically the unhealthiest species on the planet. Definitely something must be wrong with our mind

101

as most of our illnesses and mental disorders are related to the mind.

Man believes he is superior to other animals and proves this in only one way: he harms them or kills them. This killing has placed many species on the danger list of survival. In his self-conceit, man sees himself as a glorious and triumphant hunter. Man, however, is not a hunter. Man is a killer.

Many people urge world governments to agree on an ecological policy which would save the planet.

But, most of the time, these governments are made up of the very people who created the ecological crisis in the first place. These governments are mainly made up of people with a strong reptilian mentality. In our culture of free competition and free corruption, in order to reach a position of power, people in governments have to be more ruthless than others. The ruthless reptilian mentality operates on the here and now basis, a basis which has neither a global concept, nor any concept of the future. Reasoning without these concepts leaves little chance of solving the ecological crisis.

These governments are mostly male dominated and do not know the first thing about nursing, nurturing or house-keeping, so essential in helping life on our planet to survive.

The main contributors to ecological pollution and environmental destruction are industrialized liberal democracies. These democracies are made and kept alive by liberal capitalism which leans on cruel or cold-blooded competition, on the ruthless exploitation of natural resources and on unscrupulous free-markets and these are all major factors of ecological problems.

In order to be able to start solving the ecological problem, humanity must change its mentality. We have to become serious, we have to evolve from the adolescent mentality into maturity. This can only be done by developing and using the humane brain.

While we are obsessed with our cult of individualism, with our cult of individual freedom and independence, with our sense of individual self-importance, with the assertion of our wishful self-made self, with the pursuit of excitements, we cannot develop needs for caring and nurturing. While we are obsessed with self-love, we cannot develop loving or nursing.

By developing our humane brain, we develop the need for caring, nurturing, loving or nursing, without which we cannot improve the conditions of our habitat or our life, in spite of the millions of dollars spent on various committees for the protection of the environment or on various save-the-planet projects.

The appeal "keep the environment clean" or "save energy" cannot be taught or absorbed by self-absorbed individual minds. A self-absorbed person does not even notice a litter bin in a public place, let alone use it.

Some people insist on creating "universalistic human solidarity".This is one of the pompous banners we like to march behind, or decorate ourselves with, in our search of individual self-importance or individual excitement. There is no human solidarity without humaneness and there is no humaneness without a well developed humane brain.

Our present culture which praises and glorifies adventures and adventurousness cannot solve the problem of the planet's future. Adventurousness is a here and now performance which seldom takes the consequences of its performance into consideration. This is why adventures are destructive.

The destructiveness of adventures are damaging as they are often caused by despair, which can lead to violence.

We are more and more attracted by ugliness and vulgarity, by violence and terror, by decomposition and destruction. We are attracted by these because the fears they provide create what we call excitements. Our art and literature, our theatres and films, deal more and more with these subjects. The more we are attracted by ugliness and vulgarity, by violence and terror, by decomposition and destruction, the less we are able to care about the quality of our habitat or the quality of our life and even less about the lives of any other species.

We are already in a vicious circle. The increase in

population coupled with the decrease in natural resources, increases poverty. In order to decrease the poverty, humanity needs to increase economic growth. Increasing economic growth, produces more problems for the ecology and a higher exploitation of natural resources on the expenses of the future.

In order to solve this problem, some people have invented another wishful ideology: "sustainable economic growth." This means economic development which meets the needs of the present without compromising the conditions which will allow future generations to meet their needs.

The negative side of this new ideology is that it has been invented by people with the same mentality which created the problem. What is more, this "sustainable economic growth" would be planned and run by individuals more interested in their own self-interest than in the interest of those in need. This will create a situation in which the rich become richer and the poor, poorer. People who would run the planning of the "sustainable economic growth" belong to the mentality which operates an instant or a short-term expediency, unable to visualize long-term planning.

We have seen communist economic planning, which was invented and run by a similar mentality, producing economic and ecological disasters.

This should not be surprising as economic plans are invented and executed by our present mentality, a mentality based on the cult of individual self-interest, more concerned with the present than the future. When a self-centred individual who is guided by his cult of self-interest takes the notion of the future into consideration, it is to relate the future to his self-interest of the present and not the future for the future's interest.

Some people insist that it would help to solve our ecological crisis if humanity started acquiring an individual sense of responsibility inspired by ecological consciousness or awareness.

This is another wishful fantasy of the mind. With its cult of individualism, of individual freedom and autonomy, our culture creates emarginated individuals, frightened in their isolation and loneliness. To pretend from a frightened individual to have an individual sense of responsibility, however the ecological cause might be noble, is not knowing the effects of fears on our senses and perception, on our reasoning and behaviour. An individual responsibility implies choice. In fear there is no such a thing as choice. In fact, most of our ecological destruction is not a result of individual irresponsibility, but a result of the innocence of those under compulsory behaviour ruled by fears. In here and now reasoning and activities there is no room for a sense of individual responsibility.

Humanity could help to start solving the ecological problems by creating a globally valid Charter of Ecological Rights.

If we intend to preserve nature it would be only logical to entitle nature with its natural rights. This Charter should represent the rights of future generations. It should be logical that future generations and their rights should be represented in the present, as their survival is related to the activities and attitudes of the present generation.

Obviously, this Charter of Ecological Rights should include animal rights to their lives and the survival of these species.

This Charter should be above the Charter of Human Rights, as certain human rights of the present generation positively damage both the human and animal rights of future generations.

The supreme duty of the present generation should be to pass to future generations at least the same, if not a better world than that they inherited from previous generations. The chapter of Ecological Rights should, in fact, carry the wise guide-line of the American Indians which stresses that "we have not inherited the earth from our parents, we have borrowed it from our children."The present generation is passing more and more debts and a more and more overcrowded and polluted planet, to the next.

This Charter of ecological Rights should be above the present Church or State laws or moralities. This is justified as the very essence of ecology implies survival. The

Pope does not take into the consideration the survival of future generations of humans with his obsessive prohibition of birth control. The Pope should realize that many conceptions are undesirable side effects of man's pursuit for orgasmic pleasures. The preservation and the expansion of the Catholic species should not continue on the expenses of other human and animal species.

Each country should have a Committee in charge of the Charter of Ecological Rights. The representatives of this committee should be mainly mothers as they are naturally more maternal towards the ecology and to future generations.

There is no way of solving the ecological crisis if ecology is not a major factor of the economy. Each board of every company in all industries should have a representative from the committee looking after the Charter of Ecological Rights. No production of any kind should be allowed without calculating and compensating the ecological cost of that production. This ecological cost should be calculated on local and global levels.

No law of national parliaments should be valid without the approval of the committee in charge of the Charter.

This committee should not allow budget deficit or any public borrowing. Budget deficits and public borrowing imply a life on the credit of the present generation to be paid by the next generation.

The honesty and decency of life on credit can be deduced from the following text, written by that great champion of budget deficits and public spending, J.M.Keynes: "We repudiate entirely customary morals, conventions and traditional wisdom. We were, that is to say, in the strict sense of the term, immoralists....We recognized no moral obligation, no inner sanction, to conform or obey...So far as I am concerned, it is too late to change. I remain and always will remain an immoralist."

Priority in budget balancing should be given on military expenses. The reduction of military power can only contribute to a reduction of aggressiveness. A reduction in aggressiveness would increase the potential for cooperation.

By eliminating inflation, the elimination of budget deficits and the elimination of public borrowing would stabilise national currencies, reducing the threat from the speculators of the international money markets. This is of a major importance because no government in the world can govern its country and its country's economy under the constant threat of the massive power of international speculators.

The Charter of Ecological Rights should be a subject of study in all schools. This would help the young to also acquire a notion of the future.

Ecological tribunals should be introduced. These would deal with crimes against the environment, crimes against life, against life's survival.

At the beginning of this book I stressed that the Great Designer of life on our planet was its ecological conditions. Any damage against these conditions must be considered a crime against life.

Like the rest of the judiciary system, these ecological tribunals should be run by mothers as they have a better developed humane brain, which has a well developed need for caring, housekeeping and tidiness. There is no justice without fairness. Implying humaneness, fairness can only be exercised by the humane brain.

The Charter of Ecological Rights should have a special chapter dealing with science. No scientific project or research should be made without the approval of the committee in charge of the application of the Charter. No project should be approved without being accompanied by the precise cost of the project's consequences on life and on the environment.

Science can be either inspired by the mind or by the humane brain. It is the science inspired by the human mind and by our present culture and mentality that is the major contributor to the ecological crisis. This is because the mind's inspired science is used to prove the mind's beliefs rather than to improve the conditions of life on the planet.

107

The mind's inspired science is used by the mind in order to help the mind more in search of power and dominance, than to serve mankind.

Any new scientific discovery increases our sense of importance as we consider ourselves a part of the nationality which was able to realise such a discovery.

In order to reduce people's sensitivity to their real problems, governments often build glamourous prestige projects. These projects increase people's sense of importance and their infatuations which reduces sensitivity and common sense reasoning. Billions of dollars of national and global resources have been spent on futile but glorious space adventures by Soviet Russia and the USA.

Increasing people's sense of importance and conceit, however, prestige projects also increase people's expectations. The higher the expectations, the higher, too, the disappointments. One thing is steadily increasing with scientific progress: people complaining, Behind complaints lies the pretension that we deserve more or better, or both.

Our present science is aggressive and destructive because it serves the mind's wishful abstractions and, above all, because it is inspired by the mind's belief in its superiority to nature.

"Quod est ergo ratio?" meaning, what is wisdom or rationality, Seneca asked. "Naturae imitatio," he answered. The mind considers itself above this wisdom.

Our science is aggressive because the mind puts faith into it. Faith operates in the destructive black or white, good or evil way.

Being a faith, science tends to expand. Sooner or later expansion ends in over-expansion. It seems that we have already reached this stage: our science seems to have gone far beyond our needs.

This should not be surprising as with the mind the major drive of our attitudes and behaviour, our biological need, is replaced by the mind's desire, by its wish, aiming at proving the mind's validity and its ego's importance. Desire, or the need of the mind, has priority over our biological needs in this world dominated by the mind. The negative side of desire is that it tends to expand into greed with its gratification, while need diminishes with satisfaction. The gratification of desire tends to expand because it increases our sense of importance which increases our pretensions.

What is more, instead of serving humanity, the mind's science has become a new divinity. The mind's science has become scientism which implies a blind confidence in science's omnipotence. This also implies that instead of helping us to acquire a critical rationality and reasoning, our present scientism pretends worship and obedience from us. Instead of illuminating us, our scientism is bringing us into darkness. It brings us into darkness because it frightens us and this reduces the efficiency of our sense, our perceptions and our reasoning.

There are positive signs that in its over-expansion, our science has entered a phase of explosion. The main characteristic of explosion is that it is unable to control itself, or to control the side-effects of its behaviour. In my view, our science entered the phase of its explosion with the explosion of the first atomic bomb on Hiroshima.

Other positive signs that science has reached the irresponsible state of explosion is the nuclear terror that it created. We also live on a toxic bomb created by the increasing dumping of nuclear waste all around the world. Obsession with genetic manipulation is another sign of the irresponsible explosion of our science.

Instead of reducing our fears and anxieties, our science has increased them. Even its elitist jargon aims at the intimidation of mortals. Fears, anxieties and intimidations created by our present science bring a form of learned barbarianism, the practice of scientific cruelty or sophisticated atrocities,

The mind's science is mainly based on speculative hypotheses. Hypotheses are preceded in the mind by the mind's frames, by its pre-existing wishful beliefs or preconceptions, or by an inflated ego in search of self-importance, usually by both.

The discoveries of the mind's science must be in tune with the pre-existing world of the mind, often pleasing it and its ego. This prevents the mind's science from reaching an objective truth. The mind's science can provide

109

a subjective truth, but which consists of a belief in a personal truth. Our culture is mainly based on these subjective truths. It is these truths which are the major contributor to the ecological crisis.

The mind's science works in tune with the mind's wishful purpose and the science which operates with a purpose is not real science. It is not real, because, working in line with a purpose, it cannot provide us with the "how" of things or events. Without this "how" there is no real understanding of things or events.

How the mind's pre-existing frames, created by culture can distort scientific reasoning and hypotheses can best be seen in the glorification of the omnipotent gene. Only a mind which was framed by Judeo-Christianity and its one and only omnipotent God could have given supreme importance to a single component of a cell, when any common sense analysis can realize that a cell can only exist and survive through the cooperation of all of its organelles. It is obvious that it is the cell which activates its own genes and not vice versa. It is the environment in which a cell exists which stimulates the cell and it is the cell which stimulates its genes in tune with the environmental stimulation of the cell. This is best seen in morphogenesis and the differentiation of cells in a multicellular organism. A cell's activity and the activity of this cell's genes in a multicellular organism are determined and ruled by signals the cell receives from the neighbouring cells. It is this cooperation that produced a multicellular organism in the first place. Any independent activity of the cell or any independent activity of a gene of the cell in a multicellular organism would imply the end of the cell and often the end of the organism.

Obsessed by the cult of individualism and by the cult of the individual's selfishness and self-interest, Western science has invented the "selfish gene". Apologists of the selfish gene insist that "intragenomic conflict", this free for all ruthless competition between the genes of a genome is in the interest of the cell, of the organism and of the species. This ruthless competition between genes would be the major evolutionary force.

Obsessed by their cult of individualism and by their

110

cult of the individual's selfishness and self-interest, these people became blind in front of the evidence that the genes of a cell are in a dormant state, that they have no individual initiative and that their activities have to be started and stimulated by the cell's enzymes or hormones.

The worshippers of genes also forget that if the cell was able to survive for billions of years in more or less the same form and if it has succeeded to become the basic unit of life, it is because it operates in harmony with itself and in harmony with its environment.

If genes were selfish and competitive for power and predominance, we would never have had a cell and even less a multicellular organism. If genes were ruthlessly selfish we would not have had the same number of genes in each species' genome for so many millions of years. Selfishness implies competition and competition implies the elimination of victims. If this was true, we would now have, after millions of years of ruthless competition in each species' genome , a one and only supreme gene. If this were true, then we would not have to-day, after millions of years of ruthless elimination of the unfit genes, genetic diseases. If this was true, then all species would by now be eternal as the longevity genes would have eliminated the ageing genes.

If there was the so -called selfish gene, our species would have never developed the humane brain with its loving, caring, nursing, pity or sympathy.

When Darwin even included the human species in his theory on natural selection, based on individual ruthless competition, British culture was already dominated by Adam Smith's economics, based on ruthless individual competition. Darwin did not realise that the ruling liberal capitalism,with its cold-blooded individualism and unscrupulous individual competition, brought fears and anxieties, which brought Western humanity back to the reptilian state of existence. In fact, Darwinian theories work perfectly well on the reptilian level.

Only a mind inspired science and its culture, dominated by the cult of individualism, could have invented the so-called "Anthropic Principle", which places man in the centre of the universe.

Only a science belonging to a culture based on the

cult of individualism and the cult of individual autonomy, could have created the "Quantum Theory". This theory states that the observed does not exist without the observer and that the observer determines the observed. This is true for the observer, ruled by his mind, as he is removed from reality. A Quantum Theory observer is an outsider, far removed from the observed. The very idea of the observer could have only been created by the mind, which by its very essence and existence is detached from the real world.

I would like to add here that it is this idea of the observer that inspired the mind's idea of consciousness or awareness. In self-consciousness the observer's mind reaches the ability to observe and to notice his own reality or his mind's pretensions.

For an escapee from reality, reality is behind him. In order to see it, he has to look back from a distance. Looking back from a distance, an escapee does not see accurately, he only guesses. This opens the way to speculations, fiction or hypotheses. That is why the observed's essence and existence depends on the observer's speculative observations.

What is more, by escaping reality, an observer looks at it with animosity and fear, often with hatred and this limits the observer's objectivity.

An observer, ruled by wishful beliefs, observes the external world with the needs of the beliefs which influence perception. As I stressed before, the process of life consists of biochemical discomfort in search of a lesser discomfort. This need creates receptors and receptivity which result in perception and perceptivity for whatever can placate or reduce the discomfort. It is need which creates receptivity; it is receptivity which creates perceptivity; it is perceptivity which creates the senses and their sensitivity.

Ever since the mind started ruling our mental activity, the mind's discomfort or needs created the receptivity for whatever can placate or reduce the mind's discomfort or needs. This receptivity creates the perceptivity and sensitivity for whatever can give satisfaction to a mind in need.

An observer with a strong religious belief will see the finger of his God in whatever he observes. The

112

Anselmian motto: "Intelligo ut credam", meaning that we understand what we believe, is the motto of the mind's science. An observer with a specialised mind will see the external world through the eye of his specialisation. The mind can be so powerful that it is able to have wishful visions.

That each observer finds his own truth in the observed can best be seen in the so-called social sciences, such as anthropology, economics or sociology.

Living in the idealised world of his mind, Sartre could not but perceive that "reality is never beautiful."

The mind's science discovered the "many fold theory". This is logical for the mind's world as the mind changes from individual to individual and in the same individual in accordance with the degree of his fears of the moment. "Quot capita, tot sententiae," used to ironize the Roman satirists about human minds.

The mind's science has difficulty in finding the objective truth because of the lack of dialogue between the observer and the observed. An observer implies a detachment and detachment implies a monologue. Present science stresses that the observed is influenced by presence and observation by the observer.

The objective scientific truth, which will be less damaging to life and the environment, could only be discovered if instead of being removed from the observed, the observer was in contact with it, a part of it, if the observer listened to the observed, if they communicated with each other. A scientist guided by a caring, loving, nurturing or nursing humane brain would acquire a real knowledge of the outside world because, instead of observing the outside world from outside it, he would be part of it, he would belong to it, share it.

Only lonely and atomised individuals, products of the culture based on the cult of individual autonomy, could have started searching for atomised reality. Only the mind's science trying to prove itself, trying to become reality by raping nature, could have developed the desire to split the atom. In order to prove itself the mind's scientists helped in building nuclear power stations without having been able to calculate or even guess the risks of a potential catastrophe.

Scientists inspired by the caring or loving humane brain would have never split the atom or produced nuclear bombs. Operating with a wider dimension of time and the future, scientists, inspired by the humane brain, would have been able to foresee the consequences.

The mind's science invented and helped to create all manners of destructive weapons, inspired by fears that the mind carries with its wishful beliefs. The mind's wishful beliefs carry fears of both real and imaginary enemies. The paradox is that possessing or carrying a weapon increases fear, fear that the enemy might possess or carry the same or a better weapon. Possessing or carrying a weapon can also create a terrorizing fear that the enemy might be quicker in using his weapon.

Leaning mainly on the hypotheses of an outsider, the mind's science does not help the main purpose of life which is to reduce instability, anxieties or fears. The mind's science often misses even the very purpose of science. Leaning on its "Principle of Uncertainty", the mind's science has difficulty in foreseeing events, in providing a reliable prediction.

Being in communication with reality, being part of it, science inspired by the humane brain would be in a better position to foresee events, to predict the consequences or side effects of events. This would help in reducing our instability, our uncertainty, our anxieties and our fears.

We often hear complaints that science is responsible for much of our isolation and loneliness. Personally I think that it is the isolated and lonely mentality which created science that contributes to our isolation and loneliness. Individual isolation and loneliness started long before science was invented.

Some people complain that science has dehumanised humans. Could it not be that it is the dehumanised brain, the brain ruled by our mind and its wishful fantasies, which created and contributed to-wards dehumanising science.

Only a dehumanised brain could have invented nuclear terror, contributing to the further dehumanisation of humanity. Only a dehumanised brain can continue to pollute and destroy its own habitat, which continues to contribute to further dehumanisation or brutalisation of humanity. The steady increase in violence, crime, atrocities, vulgarities and ugliness shows how dehumanisation prospers.

Dehumanisation contributes to an individual's isolation and loneliness which reduces our communications with the external world even more. Without communication with the external world, our hallucinations and paranoia increase.

Only a dehumanised mind's brain could have invented all manners of unnecessary gadgets and passed them on to their children in order to dehumanise them as well. We have invented all kinds of electronic toys or videos in order to enable our children to play solitary games, games in isolation from the real world.

What is more, with video games we prepare our children for a fantasy world; we are replacing reality with a "virtual reality"and are even proud of it.

Belonging to a culture dominated by the cult of self-interest and self-centredness, the mind inspired scientist commits all kinds of fraud and misconduct; he is easily corrupted as his ego is highly inflated. Many mind inspired scientists would sell their souls for grants, fame or the Nobel prize. In fact, it is this avidity which limits long term rationality or humaneness in most scientists.

In our culture, science enjoys the reputation of importance. This is why it attracts a human element desperate for importance, people with highly pretentious egos.

That mind inspired science attracts people with highly inflated egos is evident from the fact that most scientists lack common sense and a sense of humour. Taking ourselves over-seriously kills common sense and a sense of humour.

Many people reproach women for providing relatively few scientists. I hope that the above explanation might explain why women are less obsessed with their sense of self-importance and with their individual egos.

Carrying a brain with the need for nursing and nurturing, women are less aggressive and less destructive towards nature and natural order. Only women imitating men would have split the atom or created nuclear terror.

Knowledge acquired through the mind's science is mainly based on theses, hypotheses and speculations which does not help our precariousness very much and even less our understanding of nature. Strong evidence of this is our destruction of nature.

In fact, it would be far better for our habitat and for life on our planet if we had no knowledge rather than having the knowledge provided by the mind inspired science. Scientific knowledge inspired by the mind tends to reinforce the mind's beliefs and ideologies, making them more aggressive and more arrogant. Nazi Germany is a good example where scientific knowledge resulted in helping and serving Nazi ideology and its atrocities.

With the mind's pretension to prove itself through domination, man developed an exceptional desire for knowledge in the hope that it would help him in his pretension. In fact, our desire for knowledge, our mind's need for knowledge, has gone far beyond our real need for it.

Parents strive to send their children to the best schools to acquire maximum knowledge, to help them achieve successful lives. On the other hand the same parents and the same schools try to inculcate in them cults of individual autonomy, individual competition and individual assertion. The more we succeed in the materialisation of these cults, the more we are under the influence of our reptilian legacy, the more we practice ruthless selfishness and cold-blooded brutality. The more we are guided by here and now gratification, the enemy of long term rationality and a wider way of reasoning, the more we will damage our future and that of our planet.

What a ridiculous paradox. We acquire knowledge in order to pursue irrationalities better. This paradox reaches pathetic proportions when we see highly knowledgeable people trying to destroy each other.

Our culture, based on wishful beliefs and cults, is the major source of a distorted knowledge which provides a special ignorance, a damaging and destructive ignorance, the ignorance of believers, the ignorance of those who believe they know best. A believer's knowledge is dangerous and destructive because it is aggressive. It is aggressive because it is partisan. The knowledge of a believer is chosen to serve his beliefs. A believer in free-market capitalism and its ruthless competition believes to know that the outside world is a Darwinian jungle or Hobbes' war of all against all.

A believer's knowledge is dangerous because it is both blind and stubborn. It is this blindness and stubbornness of a believer's knowledge that is responsible for a great deal of the ecological pollution and destruction. For the pretentious minded scientist, the environment's only purpose is to serve his science. That is why most scientists are annoyed by environmentalists. The mind's science is a faith and faith considers whoever or whatever is against it, an enemy.

Our present culture considers scientific innovation as progress. We are obsessed with scientific innovations. This obsession prevents us from seeing the damage this progress has on ecology.

Progress implies novelty. Novelty causes excitement, excitement created by fear of the unknown. In this excitement, which limits our reasoning, we do not analyze the effects or side effects that the novelty might produce on our habitat and the life in it. When we notice these effects or side-effects, it is usually too late as the damage is often irreparable.

The excitement of scientific progress inhibits adjustment and consolidation. This increases anxieties and stress. In fact, with the advancement of progress, stress related diseases and mental disorders also advance.

Scientific progress tends to lean on quantitative values more than on qualitative ones and any quantitative growth decreases harmony and symmetry, the sources of quality and beauty.

The supreme aim of scientific progress is power and domination. Power however, increases fear both for those who are under it and of those who possess it. That those who are in power live in fear can be seen by the desperation employed to increase it and to exercise it in order to prove it. Power is damaging. Power cannot be rational. In order to be rational it would stop growing or proving itself, which would be the end of it.

As the purpose of life is to reduce its instability and its fears and as power brings instability and fears, scientific progress, which helps power, seems to be contrary to the main purpose of life.

In its obsession for growth, scientific progress accelerates the rhythm of life, which puts more and more strain on the natural rhythm of the biosphere.

EITHER MATURE OR PERISH

We are becoming more and more aware that our present culture and mentality are frivolous and that we live life too adventurously.

Many people are slowly realising that we have reached the moment to face the problems of our planet and the life on it more maturely.

Some are attempting to organise world governments to try and face the crisis caused by over population, the greenhouse effect, pollution, over-exploitation of limited natural resources, the reduction of drinking water and fertile land, increasing poverty and starvation, the rapidly growing population of the elderly and the rapidly increasing crime and violence. But, as I said before, these problems are unsolvable with our present mentality because it is this mentality which created these problems and which continues to create them. Politicians, economists and ecologists behave like interior decorators with different tastes trying to decorate a house. They spend all their time fighting each other about how best to arrange the furniture in the various rooms, without realising that the shape of the house is wrong in the first place.

It is becoming increasingly obvious that we must either change our mentality or perish. The difficulty is that the main change has to be performed by man. Asking man to evolve towards maturity and seriousness means asking him to abandon his exciting adolescent mentality, to renounce the culture created by him, for him, around him and around his pretensions and sense of self-importance. Asking man to abandon his excitements and fun for serenity and wisdom, asking him to renounce his exhilarating and intoxicating cult of individualism for the spirit of the community, is like asking a drug addict to renounce to his addiction.

What is more, having lived a life created by the adolescent mind and its culture based on wishful beliefs for ten thousand years, man has a problem envisaging any other form of life or reasoning.

My ideas might attract a number of women and

mature men. The tragedy, however, is that in our present world maturity is often considered a laughing matter. Maturity is humane and humaneness is in a minority facing the ruthless, aggressive and violent mentality of the majority.

Confronted with the dilemma, mature or perish, we will have to opt for maturity in the end. To this choice will contribute a great deal the increase in our life span and our present mentality's obsessive aspiration, which is longevity. Longevity implies old age and old age implies individual dependence on the community. The idea of longevity is influencing our reasoning and behaviour more and more. We are beginning to realise the convenience of sacrificing our individual ruthless selfishness and self-interest in the interest of the community and of renouncing our reptilian here and now gratification for the benefits or dividends of the future.

People are slowly becoming aware that persevering in our present mentality will create a serious problem with the elderly, particularly with the increasing number of infirm old people. Twenty per cent of the population of Western Europe are over sixty years old. In twenty years time a third of the population will be old, leaving less working people so badly needed to assist the welfare dependent population.

In persevering with our present selfish and self-centred mentality, serious tension or conflict between the young and the old, will become unavoidable. Recently, a young Italian who killed his parents in order to inherit their fortune and spend it in pursuit of fun and excitement, has received a shockingly high number of letters from other young people, filled with admiration and congratulations.

Persevering with our selfish and self-centred mentality we might soon have to start rationing the elderly population and even put an age-limit on longevity.

In our present culture based on the cult of individualism which implies loneliness, elderly people become even more lonely and frightened which increases their own individual selfishness and self-centredness. This increases the exploitation of their rights towards social or medical welfare. The selfishness of the young in our present culture increases the emargination of the old.

There is another reason why we must accelerate our evolution towards maturity and the humane brain reasoning. The increasing number of elderly, invalids and the chronically ill, is becoming an important voting factor in Western democracies. This fragile population is easily politically manipulated by ruthless demagogues or dictators. With the present mentality, many old or welfare dependent people adopt the motto: "Après moi le déluge."

Creating the spirit of community and a sense of belonging to it, the new humane brain's mentality creates a sense of security for both the young and the elderly. This sense of security reduces fears, which reduces tension or conflict between generations.

Most people agree that life should be more humane, more humanized.

There is only one way to humanize present life and this is to develop the potential of our humane brain. Only by developing the potential of our humane brain can we eliminate the mentality and culture created by the mind's world of wishful beliefs which bring our reptilian legacy into prominence.

Education could play a major part in the development of our humane brain. Schools on all levels are obsessed with inculcating as much knowledge as possible into their students. This might make us cleverer but not wiser.

Craving to become reality, cleverness bears anxiety, agitation, violence and aggression. With wisdom and maturity, however, we acquire serenity and the joy of living.

Our present culture's schools concentrate more on teaching than on educating. We may be able to recite the classics from world literature or to memorise significant historical dates, but we are also able to ignore our neighbours, neglect our children, forget our parents, disdain foreigners or hate those who do not agree with our beliefs.

Knowledge without wisdom can confuse. In the USA, often precursors of what will happen elsewhere, more and more people are ruled by their shrinks or therapists.

It is scientifically established that the most important period in the development of the activity of our brain is during the first five years of infancy. In fact, if we do not develop certain potentials or capacities of our superior brains in this period of our life, we have serious difficulties in developing them later.

A child can only discover and develop the potential of his humane brain if the adults in charge of his education and of his life use their humane brains. The use of the humane brain with its caring, loving, cuddling and sharing, by those in charge of a child's rearing, reduces many fears of the child. This helps the child grow out of his old reptilian brain which otherwise will dictate his behaviour and attitudes for the rest of his life. There is evidence that children reared by happy and loving parents are far less violent or aggressive and more caring and loving.

With an undeveloped or underdeveloped humane brain, a child can remain in a degree of obtuseness or autism, more reptilian than humane states of existence, for the rest of his life.

Developing the humane brain, the child develops the needs of this brain which are: loving, caring, sociality, sharing, cooperation, communication, tolerance and understanding. Gratifying these needs of the humane brain, we feel a sense of belonging, we feel a sense of protection, therefore less frightened.

Eliminating many of the basic fears that any living organism carries, the use of the humane brain, the gratification of its needs and the activity related to this gratification become a satisfaction, contentment or pleasure. They become a source of the joy of living which feeds its perpetuation on itself.

Many religions preach and try to impose some of the humane brain's activities. The difference between the Churches' moral obligations and the humane brain's activities is that the formers are condescending charitable performances, inspired by the fear of God, which create neither protective togetherness nor an intimate community or familiarity, while the latter are spontaneous needs, which through togetherness, community and familiarity, create a sharing equality. It is this sharing equality, an equality on the finishing line, which produces protection, security and humaneness.

Christian and other Churches would be more of a community if they were not inspired by timorous Gods,or did not carry moral codes or commandments.

With its need for sharing and cooperation, the well developed humane brain eliminates much of our cult of individualism, in this way eliminating a great deal of individual ruthless selfishness and unscrupulous self-interest of stressful market economy and unfair competition.

Developing our need for sharing and caring could eliminate our unscrupulous exploitation of each other much more easily than any social or political revolution. In our present mentality, revolutions revolve rather than evolve situations.

By developing our humane brain and our maturity, we will realise that the life of humanity, guided by the mind's wishful beliefs and ideologies, is a sad game of self-deceit. In fact, humanity pays for this life of self-deceit with a life of suffering, a life of hating and killing each other in the name of the mind's abstractions or in the name of pretentious beliefs of superiority. We pay this life of self-deceit by being the only species which commits suicide.

More and more people try to inculcate the cult of individual self-confidence in their offspring, particularly sons. It is, in fact, this cult of individual self-confidence which brings us to our reptilian legacy more than anything. It is this cult of individual self-confidence which is a significant contributor to our present pathetic and comic way of life.

Self-confidence is an abstract concept created by the mind, a mind's wishful encouragement to an individual, frightened in the isolation created by his individual freedom and autonomy.

Being a wishful belief, self-confidence is aggressive and this damages sociality and social relations which isolates the individual even more, increasing his fears and opening the way to a serious mental disorder, over-self-confidence.

Self-confidence finds its energy in the fear that the wishful self, might not be recognised or respected. Self-confidence does not belong to our real selves but to the wishful idealised self. Only an idealisation can be pretentious.

Being a wishful belief, thus carrying fear, self-confidence brings the self-confident into a reptilian state of existence, a state in which we become ruthless in our selfishness and self-centredness. But, what can be paradoxical, self-confidence can damage our chances to reach an objective as, being an arousal, it limits the efficiency of our senses, perception and reasoning. Self-confidence's tendency to adopt the here and now gratification, positively damages the self-confident's future and often even his present. Self-confidence is also a major source of accidents.

Carrying fear, self-confidence frightens people and this revives the reptilian legacy in them.

Self-confidence is a source of crime and violence.

It is not surprising that crime and violence belong to the world of the mind. After all, the supreme aim of the mind, its very reason for existence, is to break with the existing order, or to force this order to adapt to the supernatural world created by the mind and its inflated and righteous ego.

That self-confidence is not part of nature but a wishful creation of the pretentious mind can be seen from the fact that when it fails, it becomes ridiculous. The truth in nature can always be recognised, as, whatever happens to it, it is never ridiculous or laughable.

In the USA, a country which worships the cult of self-confidence and tries to inculcate it into their children from early infancy, seventy five per cent of the people never talk to their neighbours. Twenty six million Americans carry an offensive weapon regularly. Eighteen million Americans would kill a human being for two million dollars and sixteen per cent of those interviewed would kill their spouse for the same amount.

In the USA, this country of the cult of self-confidence, there are two hundred million weapons registered. (Population: 253.6 millions).

In the USA, a country which worships the cult of self-confidence, psychotherapists, gurus and fortune-tellers prosper. The main purpose of these therapies and therapists is to encourage Americans to believe in the cult of self-confidence.

Carrying a nervous arousal, the cult of self-confidence damages people's health. It is this nervous arousal which contributes a great deal to the over-weight problem in the USA. (Sixty one per cent of the population).

One of the most negative sides of the cult of self-confidence lies in education. In cultures which worship the cult of self-confidence, all teachers, from nursery school to university have to practice self-confidence, to assume a role of authority. The role of self-confident authority intimidates pupils or students and this can inhibit learning. Confident authoritative teaching provides more of an indoctrination than learning.

It is well known that when we are intimidated, the blood goes towards those organs needed in fight or flight rather than to the brain. In fact, neurons and particularly those of the hypocampus, which plays an important part in our learning and memory, tend to become less efficient in people living under fear or stress. During intimidation, fear or stress our organism releases an extra quantity of adrenalin and cortisol hormones which inhibit our learning abilities and the efficiency of our memory. In fact, with the continuous increase in anxieties and stress, we have more and more people with memory problems later in life.

In order to eliminate the cult of self-confidence, the new culture's nurseries should eliminate any competition or competitive games. Competition and competitive games create animosity and antagonism which increase nervous tension and this damages physical and mental health.

The new culture's nurseries should organise the education of children around play. Play is a self-stimulating activity which helps aliveness, exuberance and the joy of living, which are more in tune with children's nature than the over-seriousness of competitive games.

Play implies curiosity which is the very essence of learning. Play implies exploration and experimentation, which carry a trial and error experience, the best method to learn the truth about the real world. Above all, this is the best method how to learn not to push our luck, hopes or wishful desires over the limits of our abilities.

Play implies interaction, intimacy, togetherness, cooperation, socialisation, communication, understanding and tolerance. Above all, play implies sharing which is of supreme importance, as through sharing we learn how to reach real freedom, freedom from desires, desires which lead to the ugliest of our present characteristics: envy.

Through play we learn that these activities and attitudes provide contentment, pleasure and joy. They provide contentment, pleasure and joy because they reduce fears.

By reducing fears, these activities and attitudes, which become part of our humane brain, benefit our physical and mental health, our learning and memory.

By becoming deeper and wider, learning helps us to reach a richer participation in life. A richer participation in life helps us to discover the vastness of the beauty of life.

By reducing fears, these activities and attitudes help

us to evolve from our present reptilian individual selfishness, self-interest and self-centredness.

The new culture's nurseries should have pets. Pets can help children discover the pleasure of stroking and cuddling, a pleasure which helps to develop the humane brain's needs for nursing and caring. Being playful, pets also stimulate children's playfulness.

It is useless advising families to forbid their children to watch programmes dealing with violence on T.V. or videos. Producers of these programmes should be punished in the same way drug pushers are punished. These programmes create addicts to the dangerous drug: excitement. Excitements reduce children's ability to develop a healthy curiosity and other needs of the humane brain, leaving these children in an obtuse state of existence.

Adolescence is a phase in which we start taking ourselves and our wishful beliefs or fantasies over-seriously, which is the essence of ridicule. In fact, our present culture, which is based on these over-serious wishful beliefs and fantasies is both ridiculous and pathetic.

The only way to prevent adolescence and humanity, dominated by the adolescent mentality, of being ridiculed is to emphasize, through education, the ridiculous side of the mind's world of wishful beliefs and fantasies. The best way to do this would be to introduce a sense of humour as the main subject in schools. Nothing better than a sense of humour can bring our humane common sense into prominence.

A sense of humour is often confused with wit. The difference is that the former is benevolent, the latter is malevolent, the former belongs to the caring humane brain, the latter to the aggressive mind's world of envy and nastiness.

The importance of a sense of humour is obvious from the fact that we feel offended when someone tells us that we have no sense of humour.

The power of a sense of humour can also be deduced by the fact that it is feared more than anything else by believers. In fact, authorities based on strong beliefs or ideologies persecute those with a sense of humour.

God never laughs. As a sense of humour belongs to the loving and caring humane brain, we can deduce that our God is far from being humane. His lack of humaneness can be seen in the starvation of the majority of humanity.

The efficiency of a sense of humour against the mind's pretensions can best be seen in the fact that a sense of humour is the best therapy of mind induced psychosomatic diseases, certain cancers and above all mental disorders. As the mind and its fears and anxieties can create these diseases and disorders, in the same way the humane brain and its sense of humour can create psychosomatic and mental health.

A sense of humour could help present day humanity to reach maturity. By preventing the adolescent from falling in love with himself and his wishful self-created ego, by preventing the adolescent from escaping into the intoxicating cult of individualism and the cult of individual autonomy and loneliness, a sense of humour could prevent Peterpanism and instead acquire maturity in which to relax. A sense of humour also stimulates the activities of other centres of the humane brain.

A sense of humour is within anyone's reach. If we are able to be ridiculous, surely we are also able to not be ridiculous. The best way to prevent being ridiculous is to develop a sense of self-ridicule. In fact a sense of self-ridicule is the essence of a sense of humour. A sense of self-ridicule eliminates that terrible fear, the fear of becoming a laughing matter, the fear of becoming a loser.

In his "The Tragic Sense of Life," Miguel de Unamuno wrote: "The mortal Don Quixote, in dying, realised his own comicness and bewept his sins; but the immortal Quixote, realising his own comicness, superimposes himself upon it and triumphs over it without renouncing it..... He (Don Quixote) will triumph by making himself ridiculous. And he will triumph by laughing at himself and making himself the object of his own laughter."

We complicate our life, often transforming it into a tragedy by developing over-seriousness, which, as I said, is the very source of pathos and ridicule. If we can become over-serious, then we can also become serious by deriding our pretentious over-seriousness, by not considering ourselves indispensable. By taking into consideration that the cemeteries of the world are packed with those who considered themselves indispensable, we might lose some of this over-seriousness.

A sense of humour helps adolescents to eliminate their tendency to create problems and then dramatise them. Problems and their dramatisation appeal to the adolescent's ego. But this also limits the adolescent's joy of living, exuberance and wider participation in life. A sense of humour does more than solve problems: it dissolves them.

A sense of gratitude should be a must in the new culture, a subject of teaching and exercises in schools, particularly schools dealing with adolescents.

Gratitude helps to eliminate the mind's wishful pretensions, thus helping to eliminate unhealthy tension, eagerness, yearning and desires.

Another important subject which should be part of the humane education is humbleness. Humbleness stimulates both, in ourselves and in others the development and activities of the humane brain. Humbleness implies one of the most humane attitudes which is gentleness. The best definition of gentleness I ever heard was the explanation I received one day from a peasant in Montenegro's mountains on the difference between a hero and a gentleman. The former, he said, defends others from others, while the latter defends the others from himself, from his selfishness and self-love.

In order to help adolescents not to take the mind's world too seriously, text books on National Histories should be re-written in tune with the humane culture, re-written by an international independent committee of the United Nations. These school texts should expose the destruction and wastage of the natural resources of the past, all committed in the name of wishful beliefs and ideologies. This would reduce national pride and nationalism. Being an abstract belief, nationalism is aggressive and destructive because it craves to prove itself, to become part of space and time.

Eliminating nationalism we eliminate our fear of foreigners and eliminating this fear, we develop a wider way of reasoning, which leads to a friendly relationship with other nationalities. This could economise vast amounts of resources that each national State spends on destructive weapons. With a wider reasoning and a developed humane brain we do not need nationalism to belong to it in search of protection of our pretensions, we simply lose our pretensions.

Our present culture's history serves to perpetuate this culture. In the mind's world of beliefs and ideologies, the past must be adapted to the needs of the beliefs and ideologies in power.

Victor Hugo was right when he claimed that the result of the Battle of Waterloo was due to chance, that it might have had a different outcome had it not rained the night before. Anglo-French relations would have been better had their national histories emphasised the role of chance in human events.

If national histories were taught more humorously, then history would serve its purpose and even indicate some of its logic, therefore become less of a contingency. In his book "De l'humour", Georges Elgozy stressed: "If history does not teach us anything useful it is because it is expurgated of humour".

These courses in a sense of humour could explain that with a less dramatised and less glorified past, the present would be happier and the future more organised.

The following lines written in a report by the coroner, after the assassination of Lord Mountbatten in Ireland, should be pasted all over the walls of offices of the United Nations: "However, I believe it necessary to stress again the great responsibility that parents and teachers of any nationality have in the way they interpret history and pass it on to the youth of the country, I believe that if history could be taught in such a fashion that it would help to create harmony among people, rather than division and hatred, it would serve this and all other nations better."

The past of every country is filled with absurdities and incongruities, caprice, short-sightedness and misunderstanding, cowardice and failure, lies and treacheries, accidents and chance. Why, then hide them?

It would help the education of adolescents if a course on the irrationality of religions was introduced. This course could use our own Judeo-Christian beliefs as an example to analyse it from a more mature point of view.

God can only exist if He is loved. In fact, God is desperate for love and lives in fear of not being loved. This fear makes him selfish, self-centred and the one and only centre of the Universe. He is cruel and ruthless with those who do not love him. He pontificates to His believers that it is only right and "just" to persecute and kill His enemies.

This obsessive self-love makes God insensitive, which prevents understanding, loving or caring. A loving God would never have allowed the religious wars, intolerance or persecution. A loving God would have never allowed the Inquisition or the tortures done in His name.

Life is a gift of God, as we are informed by the Church. How could a loving God give the gift to so many lives with hereditary diseases or genetic deformations. If life is a gift of God why then does the same God authorise his believers to kill life in His name.

Instead of giving life as a gift, a more mature God would have thought of renting or leasing life to each individual whose responsibility would be to return it in an improved state. He could ask each person to pay the rent for the leased life in the form of a contribution to life in general and the community in particular. God must know that there is no procreation or perpetuation of life without a community.

A frightened God is a fearful God. In fact, we live in fear of our God, His supreme purpose. But, living in fear of God, we cannot love Him. Like any other fear, the fear of God brings our reptilian inheritance, our selfishness, self-centredness and our self-love to the fore. After all, God creates His believers in His own image and likeness. This creates a comic situation in which selfish people pray to a selfish and insensitive God to help them realise their pretensions, which are above their merits, at the expense of their neighbours or other members of the community. Man only prays when in need of realising his inflated desires.

We pretend to love God out of fear of Him. This opens the way to expediency, hypocrisy or farce.

Inhibiting the humane brain's activities and mature behaviour with His intimidation, God is left with people ruled by their reptilian mentality. God had no choice but to organise his reptilian minded believers by giving them strict Commandments, a ferrous moral code. What the omniscient God did not realise is that morality is ignored by an individual's selfishness and self-love created by the fear of God's punishments. In fear we operate with our reptilian expediency, our instant opportunism.

Any break of God's Commandments is punished ruthlessly. The punishment is based on the "eye for an eye" principle, which is in tune with reptilian cruelty.

With the fear of punishment, God intended to obtain obedience. The great Christian believer, Pascal, stressed that: "True religion must, as a characteristic, have the obligation to love God." What Pascal did not realise is the fact that obedience reduces us to infancy, a state of extreme self-centredness thus unable to listen to God's Commandments.

This chronic fear of God and His punishments creates obtuseness to such a point that instead of loving our neighbours, we often do not even know their names. Living in chronic fear of God and His punishments, we develop callousness, or indifference towards compassion for those in need. Those in need might often even irritate us. In the USA, seventy per cent of the people say that they "truly" believe in God, but few of them would come out at night to assist someone screaming for help. Living in fear of God and His punishment can even create a real farce. Members of the Italian Mafia are fervent believers and often go to church and pray hard for success in the crime or murder they are planning. Many ruthless speculators pray to God, often contributing financially to the church, in order to succeed with their deals, prayers which if answered could reduce many people to miserable poverty.

Our religion also inhibits human communications. A fervent believer, communicates directly with His God, which alienates him from other humans.

These courses should also explain the irrationality of

so called "Original Sin", the penalty we pay for "Adam's fall." The purpose of punishment is to correct a sinner or a criminal and to deter further sins or crimes. Punishment cannot correct a sinner who has inherited his sin, even less prevent a sin which, according to God, we are born with. If everyone took the belief in "Original Sin" with the religious fervour of a strong believer, the human species would die out. Fervent believers by rights, would stop procreating in order to prevent the greatest of all sins, the procreation of sinners.

These courses for adolescents should stress that life is rich and generous and that any religious belief or ideological infatuation limits his participation. These beliefs and infatuations makes us miserable as they reduce our enjoyment of the wealth of life. I have never read any religious or ideological holy text which inspired any joyfulness. The gravity of these texts and of those who believe in them can reach comic proportions. Believers tell you that they are happy in their beliefs. If they were happy they would be more joyful and more playful, instead of looking sad and worried. For our God and for His Church, joyfulness and laughter are satanic.

The Judeo-Christian beliefs perpetuate our present culture, already so fascinated by religious beliefs, myths, illusions, fantasies or Utopias. Karl Marx stressed that "religion is an opiate of men." Marx should have been grateful to religions, as they prepare human minds for other opiates, his own included. Only those who are able to believe in super-nature could have been seduced by Marx ' Utopia. Religions create Homo credulus, easily manipulated by illusions.

Our God understood that those who believe in Him are discontented or in a despair created by believers' wishful pretensions. In order to keep His believers under his spell, God invented the best food for wishful pretensions: hope and promises. In the Christian religion after all, hope is a virtue.

In essence, the only realisation of hope is the

preservation and perpetuation of wishful pretensions, which help God to perpetuate His seduction. Only pretentiousness can be seduced.

Hope is a sad phenomenon. Hope keeps the hopeful away from reality. What is more, the hopeful develop fear or anxiety that the hope might not be realised. This fear or anxiety reduces the efficiency of the hopeful's senses, perception and reasoning which limits the hopeful's ability to realise his hope. Ardent hope annihilates any chance to realise hope. Contrary to many people's belief, ardent hope can limit and even prevent recovery from illness.

Being created by pretensions, hope increases credulity which can be easily manipulated by lies, propaganda, publicity or promises.

These courses should explain that any dream based on illusions or promises results in nightmares, that those who promise paradise are those who realise hell.

These courses should explain another fallacy. Our Church insists that suffering can bring redemption. Suffering in fact, brings us to our reptilian legacy which is miles from the redemption.

The Christian Church tortures us by emphasising that Jesus Christ died in agony on the cross for our sake. We did not ask Christ to die for us. Even He did not want to do it. It was His Father, God the Almighty, who insisted that he should die on the cross. A father who asks his son to sacrifice his life is not a humane father. Any mother, if she is not imitating man, would never send her child to die for an abstract cause.

Our Church would only have a meaning if its God was more maternal than paternal.

Using a sense of humour, these courses could help adolescents to avoid being seduced by the major pride of our culture based on abstractions: philosophy.

The pretentious and presumptuous aim of philosophy is to find the so-called "transcendental truth", which is a contradiction in terms. It is a contradiction in terms because it is a speculation created by the mind in its escape from reality. A speculation tends to lean on the wishfulness of the speculator. The very essence of wishfulness is to create its own truth, which, in essence, is a belief, therefore far removed from the objective truth. An objective truth belongs to the real world, a world from which man's adolescent mind escaped because the truth of the real world did not flatter the mind's pretentious and presumptuous ego and its fantasy world of imagination.

Philosophers pretend to find "higher levels of reality." In reality there are no levels of reality. Levels of reality belong to the mind's imagination, which develops with the mind's escape from reality. Fears which an escapee carry, reduce the efficiency of his senses and perception, which helps the imagination. In its expansion this imagination can reach pathological extremes.

The mind's so-called superior levels of reality are the very source of ridicule. In fact, when we topple from the mind's world to the one true reality we provoke laughter.

Even more farcical is philosophers' pretentiousness when they give us their ethical laws or their moral codes based on their transcendental truths. Having his own personal transcendental truth, each philosopher has his own ethical laws or his own moral codes. The ridiculous side of all this is that we often go to war in the name of these transcendental truths in order to kill each other. This can enable future generations to laugh at us and realise how stupid we were, if they are not intoxicated by similar transcendental truths.

Some people might claim that philosophising is healthy exercise for the brain. This is not true because philosophising is an exercise of the mind and not of the brain. On the contrary, the exercise of the mind goes against the activities and exercises of the brain. The stronger the mind and the stronger its beliefs, the more exposed the brain is to atrophy or another disorder. In fact, many philosophers lived their entire lives or ended them in madness.

What is even more pathetic and ridiculous is the fact that many of these ethic or moral beliefs created by philosophers' minds are inspired by nostalgia towards the humane brain from which the human mind escaped in search of the intoxicating and exciting world of wishful fantasies.

After twenty six centuries of philosophising, philosophers have reached a nonsense in which man is an alien for his alienated observer, in which a dehumanised observer is trying to dehumanise the observed. This is done in modern philosophy by destroying the observed, in order to build on his corpse the transcendental truth. The philosopher-observer has to kill man in order to replace him with his mind's ideal man which is made in his own image. The absurdity of this attitude can be seen if we visualise for a moment the whole world made up of philosophers. Nothing would change as each philosopher would present himself as the ideal man.

Modern philosophy reached its climax and its fall in its capital: Paris in the Sixties. In its apotheosis, modern philosophy gave the impression of a mental and verbal pyrotechnic, very much in tune with the Parisian rococo facades.

In its fall, modern philosophy acquired the main characteristic of the modern times: speed. In its vertiginous disappearance, modern philosophy left the French and world intellectuals, with the disappointment of children who had broken their favourite toy.

Post-modern intellectuals and philosophers alienated themselves from the real world even more by inventing their own esoteric language and terminology. A waiter in one of the cafes in Paris where the postmodernists often met, told me that these intellectuals are like Basques. "They talk to each other but I do not believe that they understand each other," he explained. I go further than that, these people do not even hear each other. Their egotism is so strong that it limits the efficiency of their sense of hearing.

After twenty six centuries of playing an important role in Western culture, philosophy leaves us with its message that there is no reality and that there is not an objective truth about anything. In essence, we could not expect any other finding from a humanity which lives beyond reality and is even proud of it.

These courses for adolescents should underline the importance and value of the family. Adolescents tend to consider themselves emancipated or liberated when they are able to escape the family.

Fearing ill health, adolescents should learn that family life is the best preventative and creative therapy for psychosomatic diseases, stress related illnesses and mental disorders. The family is also the best therapy against juvenile crime and violence and above all against rapidly increasing juvenile suicide.

These courses should advise and prepare students to develop hobbies. Hobbies help playfulness and joyfulness, which eliminate over-seriousness. Some hobbies, such as sailing or gardening, can contribute enormously to the development of the humane brain. Sailing and gardening, for example, teach us that we cannot go against nature and its laws in the name of desires, pretensions or super-nature.

Hobbies will also help in the post capitalist economy as this will encourage the sharing of work, which will imply a significant reduction of working hours for the individual worker.

THE NEW CULTURE

The new culture could give a major social, moral and financial importance to education and teachers.

Taking into consideration that education and the experiences of a child in the first five years of his life are of radical importance in the development of a child's brain's activities, the position and treatment of mothers and nursery school teachers should be completely changed.

Every mother should spend the first five years of her child's life with him. She should receive a salary from the State or the community during this period. The salary should be high in order to pay a particularly high respect to the most important activity in the life of a social species without well developed innate patterns of behaviour, which activity is the rearing of children, the preparation of a future citizen and worker, a husband or wife, a parent of the future humanity.

The respect of a mother's work and its high remuneration should be an important incentive to mothers to be more maternal, to be freer in the use of their humane brains.

There is evidence that children with a happy relationship in their early infancies with their mothers are happier in life and better equipped to cope with it. There is also vast evidence that those who have had an unhappy infancy are more inclined to be involved in crime and violence, obtuseness or mental disorders.

Contrary to present culture's tendency to dedicate more attention to the education of boys, the new culture's education should give equal importance to the education of girls. In many countries people's sayings stress that if you educate a male you educate one person, if you educate a female you educate a family.

Another major change of the new culture should be to place teachers on the highest level of the community's salaries. It is the teachers, from nursery schools to universities, who form and develop the brain and its mental activities for future humanity.

Paying the highest salaries to those contributing to

the education of future humanity can give the State or the community the possibility to chose educators among the most humane humans, the more mature and most maternal human element. Giving these educators respect, importance and privileges, the State or the community opens the way to a more civilised society, to a more humane humanity. A culture, like the present one, which gives importance and remuneration to films stars, pop singers, footballers, tennis players, snooker players and Olympic medallists, is not a serious culture. A culture which worships those who have made money, no matter how illegally, ruthlessly or vulgarly, is not a good culture.

The high salaries of vocations or professions contributing to the development of the humane mentality and its values should be financed by the high income tax imposed on the profit of the above mentioned people. Extra income tax on these people, mainly on popular entertainers, is justified by the fact that it is the public which makes them popular and rich. What is more, an extra high income tax on these people could bring some of these talents towards more humane and humanitarian professions and activities.

In fact, a differentiated fiscal policy, based on the degree of the activity's contribution to the development or the perpetuation of humane values, should be the main instrument in the hand of the legislator in the consolidation of the new culture and the new mentality.

This differentiated fiscal policy should be established by the legislator of the State or the community in collaboration with the authorities dealing with education, economy and justice and with the representative of the Charter of Ecological Rights. A culture based on humane values can only be realised if justice, economy and the environment were more humane.

An appropriate fiscal policy could also consolidate the family, this important unit of our social species.

For a long time, businessmen, bankers, stock-market dealers and property speculators have been able to convince the public that they deserved the highest remunerations and salaries in the community because they were creating economic wealth. In fact, they are those mainly responsible for our ecological crisis and economic uncertainty. But, even if it was true that businessmen, bankers, stock-market dealers and property speculators contributed to economic growth, we must realise that there are also other values which are more important than economic growth. It is this obsession with the economic growth of Western culture which has created the present economic and ecological crisis, starvation in many countries and a very poor quality of life. America, the wealthiest country in the world, is also the richest in crime, violence, poverty, suicides, over-weight, lawyers and psychotherapists.

The economic justification of the high salaries paid to educators can be found in the fact, that by creating a more humane humanity, the State and community would economise on the cost for fighting crime and violence, the maintenance of prisons and repairs due to the destruction and pollution of the environment. Above all, with the new culture and value, the community and the State would economise on the expenses of health care of those suffering from stress related diseases, mainly caused by the uncertainty that the mind's world of wishful beliefs carries.

As our present culture dominated by the mind's wishful beliefs is able to create psychosomatic or stress related diseases, the new culture, organised by maturity around humane values could provide psychosomatic health and a joy of living. Each culture has its own health and its own diseases. The World Health Organisation defines health as "A state of complete physical, mental and social well-being, not merely the absence of disease and infirmity." With culture based on those values in tune with the humane brain, we have a better chance of reaching this definition of health.

The most important contribution to the community's economy, however, will be the new culture's reduction or elimination of our present mental disorders, as many of these disorders belong to the mind's world of wishful illusions, which are reduced or eliminated by maturity. Our present culture takes mental disorder over-seriously, which places our culture into a ridiculous position, as over-seriousness is not serious. In fact, being based on over-serious wishful beliefs and ideologies, the whole of our present culture could be considered a farcical mental disorder. This mental disorder shows its real nature in the ideological or religious wars, persecutions or revolutions, of which we are often even proud. What we call mental disorder is, in essence, a degree above the normal of our usual pretentiousness, self-love, self-interest and self-centredness. I am sure that if a rational being from out of space saw us, he or she would report back to their planet that we are a dangerously mad species as we are destroying not only our habitat but also that of other species, in the name of wishful pretensions.

In order to explain my theory better, I would like to analyse certain mental disorders, which are increasing with the increase of pretensions which tend to increase with the increase of so-called progress. In the USA, for example, twelve per cent of the population is affected by a serious mental disorder.

Some of the following symptoms are generally associated with mental disorders: excessive selfishness and self-centredness, intolerance, impatience and insensitivity, lack of empathy or sympathy, lack of playfulness and sense of humour, lack of caring, loving or sharing, lack of flexibility or adaptability, here and now logic and an instant gratification.

These symptoms and characteristics are mainly related to our reptilian brain and to our neuro-endocrine activity which come into prominence with fears or anxieties. It is living dangerously in the precarious uncertainty of the mind's pretentious beliefs, that creates most of our mental disorders.

Mental disorders are mainly caused by the mind's wishful belief that our self-made inflated self is entitled to our excessive self-love, our ruthless selfishness, our unlimited self-centredness and above all the fulfilment or gratification of our wishful self and its desires.

In search of vast profit, the powerful industry and those who serve it, are desperate to relate these mind caused mental disorders to the biochemical activity of the brain.

They have no material interest to take into consideration that the biochemical activity of the brain can easily be caused and perpetuated by a mind's fixation or belief. After all, if the mental disorders of our species were caused by the brain's chemistry, then our cousins, chimpanzees and gorillas, with a genetic difference of only one to two per cent , would suffer from the same mental disorders, besides suicide, this act of extreme mental disorder.

Obviously, each mental disorder can find its relative biochemical activity in the brain. But, as I stressed, this biochemical activity of the brain can easily be caused by the mind. To try to concentrate on research for drugs to cure the symptoms, instead of something to prevent the cause, means not only the perpetuation of the problem but also the aggravation of the body due to the side effects of the drugs prescribed.

A nervous breakdown usually hits those who sink into a state of hopelessness. A sense of hopelessness is mainly caused by excessive hopefulness.

Statistics show that single people are more liable to nervous breakdowns. Delving deeper, statistics might prove that single people are single because of their selfishness and pretentiousness, as these prevent communication, integration and togetherness.

Phobias are mainly developed by the fears which our mind creates when it escapes from reality into excessive self-importance.

People suffering from agorophobia explain that they fear public places. This fear is secondary to an agorophobic's main fear, the fear that in public places people might deride his exaggerated self-importance.

Behind kleptomania there usually lies an excessive degree of self-righteousness.

Psychiatry explains that hysteria is a "body language", a reaction to stress caused by an "intolerable life situation."

Obviously, we place ourselves in an intolerable life situation whenever our pretentious ego places itself above the capabilities of our real self.

Hypochondriasis is mainly caused by excessive self-concern, inspired by exaggerated self-appreciation.

142

"Depression is suffered by people who see no reason to like themselves at all"..... "Depression is a state of self-hate," wrote an English authoress, who ended her own life in a moment of depression.

What kind of people see no reason to like themselves?

Those who develop a feeling of worthlessness, a feeling which is reached whenever we realise we are unable to achieve our ideals or aspirations. We can never achieve our ideals or aspirations if they are inspired by excessive self-admiration or over-ambition.

We only feel sorry for ourselves when we develop exaggerated self-adulation.

We develop "self-hate" when we are disillusioned by our self-love and we are bound to be disillusioned by self-love if we stretch it too far.

The feeling of worthlessness can easily be eliminated by developing our humane brain which replaces self-love with loving and caring for others. People who love those who need them are never depressed; people who love those that their self-love needs are always depressed.

Fears created by an escape into self-love evoke negative and frightening experiences from the memory, which contributes to the
depression by transforming dreams into nightmares.

Living in a highly precarious and uncertain state, a depressive's ego is often even threatened by non existent or trivial threats. A common cold, or biological uneasiness due to disharmony in water metabolism caused by a full moon, can increase depression in a depressed person.

By developing the humane brain and maturity, a great deal of the planet's wealth, consumed in Western countries for tranquillisers, anti-depressants or sleeping pills, would be economised.

Following today's attitude of psychiatry, psychosis is the result of a maladjusted person's escape from a hostile and uncooperative external world.

The maladjustment of a paranoiac is not caused by a hostile and uncooperative world, but by shattered expectations, expectations inspired by his ego's grandiosity. A paranoiac does not escape from reality as his mind's world, its culture and values are already far removed from reality, but from frustrated illusions into a world of bigger illusion. In their over-expansion, illusions become delusions. The world of delusions is a world of extreme fears which inhibit the efficiency and the accuracy of the paranoiac's sense of perception and this contributes to his misunderstanding or mis-interpretation of the external world.

Schizophrenia is considered as a double or split personality. Our world of the mind dominated by wishful beliefs and ideologies, illusions and hopes, pretensions and desires, is a schizophrenic world. In this world, dominated by fears, each of us can have not double but multiple personalities. Each degree of fear has its own personality. Extreme fears create extreme behaviours and attitudes. Even a mature person, guided by his highly developed humane brain, can reach a schizophrenic level of existence if a fear or a drug has reduced the efficiency of the humane brain.

Our culture imposes a cultural or theatrical personality which we have to perform in public in order to appear normal.

Some experts explain that today's impersonal city life drives more and more people towards schizophrenia. Could it not be that material progress, labour-saving gadgets of modern civilization, consumption on credit (therefore above our means) and city life, flatter an individual's ego to the point of conceit and excessive expectations, all of which increase fears and uncertainty? It is far easier to develop conceit and excessive expectations in a large city than in a small village. In a village conceit and excessive expectations are quickly derided. In the city we can live in comparative anonymity which protects our self-deceit and illusions.

Many psychiatrists claim that the best way to cure a schizophrenic is to try and restore his "self-esteem", which has been lost in his "maladaptation". A schizophrenic does not lack self-esteem; on the contrary, he has often forced it to a level of "folie de grandeur". No schizophrenics suffer from an excess of humility, humbleness, loving, caring or humaneness.

What our culture considers mental disorders or madness, are, in reality, nothing but excesses of the beliefs or fantasies of the mad world of the mind in which we live. One of the clear evidences of the madness of our mind's world is the fact that we are easily seduced by absurd ideas or utopian promises. History proves this fact. Our history is mainly made by a succession of periods dominated by absurd ideas or wishful beliefs. Recently, Russia closed one of her historic periods, discovering, after seventy years, that it was dominated by ideas that could have only been created by people suffering from mental disorders.

With its "holy" wars and brutal killings, all in the name of ideologies, our history is the best evidence that our past and our present are results of the human mind's mental disorders. We are even proud of our past which is yet another proof of our madness. One of the main characteristics of mental disorder is a lack of shame.

Living in a world dominated by ideas created by mental disorders, we do not find it mad, shameful or ridiculous to proclaim a building as sacred, to go there and prostrate ourselves in front of dead objects and to pray for things we cannot obtain with our talents or abilities. In order to obtain things we do not deserve, we develop another madness: belief in miracles, in events which are contrary to natural laws. We do not laugh at this pretentiousness which has transformed us into a begging species. We would, however, if we saw a group of sardines in a grotto, prostrate in front of a dead sardine crucified on a cross.

Our present culture's madness can also be seen in the absurdities of modern and post-modern art, mainly concentrated on deforming reality. This madness becomes even more prevalent with people who try to explain the greatness of abstract art, particularly when people are actually prepared to invest vast amounts of money in this art.

By developing the humane brain, we could save many resources and reduce much suffering, in the field of certain serious physiological disorders of the brain.

There are more and more old people to-day. More and more of them suffer from loss of memory and Alzheimer's disease.

There is a positive evidence that the wishful world of

145

the mind influences the brain's neuronal activity and the activity of the neurotransmitters and above all the activities of the cells and the neurotransmitters of the limbic brain which plays an important role in memory.

Could it not be possible, that Alzheimer's disease and various other problems with memory, are caused, at least in part, by our culture, by our mind and its beliefs or preconceptions? After all, each culture has its own diseases and disorders. Could it not be that problems of the memory are caused by a reduced efficiency or even atrophy of the brain's cells that deal with the memory?

Like the atrophy of any cells, atrophy of the brain's cells usually takes place when the cells are poorly exercised. The mind's rigid beliefs or strong prejudices can form a kind of fixed framework in our brain, which could easily reduce the activity of the brain's cells which are not part of the fixed frames. These frames could reduce the efficiency and exercise of the brain's cells dealing with curiosity, alertness and interest. These frames also reduce emotions and the graduation in emotional states which in turn reduce the activity and vibrations of the cells dealing with memory.

In my long research, I noticed that a great number of those suffering from poor memory or Alzheimer disease were people who had lived their lives guided by strong single-track minds, people who based their lives on narrow-mindedness, on rigid beliefs, on rigourous prejudices, on fixed ideas, on strong social rules, on fashion or routine-imposed mental attitudes. This narrow-minded brain's activity which limits curiosity and an interest in anything which is beyond the mind's preconceptions, seems to limit the activity and vibrations of the brain's cells producing certain neurotransmitters, particularly of the brain's cells secreting acetylcholine, which seems to play an important part in the memorisation of new events and in the revocation from the memory of past events. This reduced curiosity or interest perhaps reduces the activity of the enzymes or proteins which help the production and activity of the acetylcholine and of other neurotransmitters, so important in the memorisation and use of the memory. There is a positive evidence, however, that poor use of neurons diminishes the activity of the nerve growth factor which is important in the activity of the brain's cells.

It is easily noticeable that, being more outgoing, more curious and more interested in others than in themselves, people with well developed humane brains, people who need to care, love or share, people with a sense of humour, seldom develop problems with their memories.

With a better developed humane brain we could greatly improve our communications. Better communications create closer togetherness, sociality and the spirit of the community and this reduces uncertainties, anxieties and fears. Reducing uncertainties, anxieties and fears, we widen our brain's activity and intelligence, which provides a richer and more detailed mental picture of the world, which reduces both the unknown and the fear of it.

Improving intelligence and reasoning, togetherness, sociality and the spirit of the community contribute to their own consolidation and to their own improvements.

A better developed humane brain, whose neuronal architecture, neuronal specialisation and neuronal interconnections took place in a more humane, in a more loving and caring climate, creates a greater need for communications. In fact, our spoken language, which distinguishes us from other animals, must have been started and developed by our ancestral mothers. Their better developed humane brain must have felt a need to communicate with their infants. Infants of our species have always been more dependent on their mothers and for much longer than infants of any other species.

Girls of to-day inherit this need to communicate. In fact, girls use the spoken language better than boys. Boys acquire it more through imitation and learning than through an innate drive. I would not be surprised if one day science discovers that the cells of Broca's and Wernicke's areas of the left lobe of the brain's cortex, which seem to be associated with the spoken language, were better developed and better organised in the human female than in the human male.

That communication is a need of woman's humane brain can be seen from the fact that when this need is gratified, she usually experiences a certain contentment or fulfilment. Being more related to his ego, man's communication is often a performance which can leave the performer in anxious doubt that he could have performed his communication with better effect.

GENDER

With a better developed humane brain, humanity could achieve a far better relationship between man and woman and this would create a more harmonious family in which the children could have a better chance to develop their humane potential , to reach maturity. In maturity there is equality between woman and man. In maturity there is no room for the gender between the sexes. In maturity, both man and woman are maternal.

"The great question that has never been answered and which I have not yet been able to answer, despite my thirty years research into the feminine soul, is : "What does a woman want?" This is a statement of Freud. If Freud was more perceptive he would have not had this problem. In order to have been more perceptive, Freud should have come down from his pedestal of egotism. A sense of self-importance limits the efficiency of sense-perception. That is why Freud could never have realised "What a woman wants? " What in essence, women really want, is to see men reach maturity.

The idea of gender is a male adolescent mind's creation. Maleness is a wishful abstraction, an ideology. Like any other wishful ideology, maleness places its believer, in the believer's eyes, into a position of superiority.

Like any other ideology, man's maleness has an imaginary enemy. Maleness' enemy is woman. In fact, it is the fear of woman that man feels in his adolescent rebelliousness that creates the maleness ideology. The enemy of an ideology has to be evil, nasty, devious, brutal or ugly, thereby perpetuating the fear of the enemy. From the philosophers and politicians of Ancient Greece and India, to Nietzsche, Freud and modern religious fundamentalists, woman was depicted in negative terms.

Like any other ideology, man's maleness craves its materialisation, it craves to prove itself. This can only be done through force and violence, arrogance and aggression, coercion or rape. An ideology finds its best materialisation

149

through the denigration, subjugation or domination of its enemy. Through the denigration, subjugation or domination of woman, man acquires the illusion of placating his fear of her.

Gender ideology is the major contributor to the widely spread phenomenon of the polarity in our present culture. Our present culture, in fact, is dominated by a permanent struggle of opposite extremes. In reasoning influenced by polarity everything tends to be either/or, or black or white. In polarity various shades of grey are a neither/nor existence.

Being influenced by the struggle of opposite extremes, our reasoning has difficulty in grasping the whole. By only seeing one side of a coin, or the other, we fail to see the coin in its globality.

A struggle of opposite extremes aims at the conqueror/conquered state of existence which creates a lasting stress for both sides. In fact, we live in a world in which man is stressed because he has to live with lies in order to keep up with his artificially created superiority and importance. Woman becomes stressed because she has to adapt herself to a life of lies, because she has to cope with life organised by man around his stressful existence.

Woman became a victim of her own superiority consisting of better adaptability to the environmental changes and external pressure. She adapted herself to man's world ruled by his prepotency. She adapted herself to the reptilian reasoning and behaviour of the majority of men. She seldom protested even when, in the name of their abstract beliefs or absurd ideologies, man sent her children to kill other mothers' children in so-called holy or just wars or revolutions.

Lately, women's adaptation to the adolescent minded male culture is taking a dangerous turn. More and more women adopt the cult of individualism and of individual autonomy which is going against their strong community oriented nature. This means more and more women living in loneliness and a fear of it, which are sources of women's restlessness, agitation, aggression and even violence. Living an artificial life, a life contrary to their very nature, more and more of these women are under stress, more and more of them are victims of stress-related diseases or mental disorders. At least half of ten percent of those suffering from insomnia in the developed world are now women. Male insomnia seems to be caused mainly by man's mind's over-activity created by man's mind's excessive expectations or pretensions. Women's insomnia, however, appears to be caused mainly by physical and mental over-exhaustion in coping or performing with an assumed role so contrary to their innate caring, loving, sharing and community-orientated nature.

Clear evidence of women's loneliness, fear and stress, caused by their imitation of man's invented cult of individualism and of individual autonomy is a steady increase in women's consumption of alcohol, tranquillisers or narcotic drugs. The longer a woman adopts the cult of individualism and of individual autonomy the more she is susceptible to becoming an alcoholic or drug addict.

Recently women have been trying to form liberation movements. In our culture dominated by wishful beliefs and ideologies, however, most of these feminist movements or attitudes become inspired by an ideology.

Liberated women insist that they want equality of the sexes. What they really want is equality of genders. This brings serious tension. The male gender is generated by the idea of superiority of man over woman. By wanting to achieve equality with man, the liberated woman wants to be superior too. The tension is caused because superiorities incline to exclude equality.

Like any other ideology, feminism brings the reptilian legacy into prominence, which increases the believer's selfishness, self-centredness, insensitivity and here and now gratification and reasoning.

Like any other ideology, feminism has its enemy: man. The negative side-effect of animosity and hostility is that they reduce and distort perception to the point that we only see what justifies and what nourishes our hostility. A fanatical feminist can see a male-chauvanist pig in every man. Another side-effect of hostility is that it tends to isolate the hating individual, which escalates the hostility, often reaching ridiculous extremes.

Like any other ideology, feminism suffers from compulsive expansion. In its over-expansion, an ideology loses its cause. In its explosion, which follows over-expansion, an ideology disintegrates or ends in violence.

The present battle of the sexes is a battle of two ideologies which is even more pathetic and ridiculous if we take into consideration that by nature we are a social and a cooperative species. We are the only social and cooperative species in which males and females are often neither social nor cooperative to-wards each other. In their ideological battle, man and woman are often able to even kill each other.

Feminism would acquire a far more realistic meaning if woman concentrated harder on helping man to reach maturity.

In the next chapter I will describe some of the measures humanity will have to accept if they want to achieve a more civilized and humane life. Helping realize these measures, women can help men to become more mature, help themselves and their children and above all save the future of the planet.

By helping woman, both biologically and mentally better equipped to survive, to be herself, man would also help himself. This is because with woman in prominence, the community and sense of community are more in evidence. Man feels safer, more protected in a community, so essential for a creature who is easily frightened and who, when frightened, panics.

Woman is entitled to care for humanity because, by nature, she is caring. Guided by his inflated wishful ego, man is only able to care for his short-term self-interest.

The main problems facing humanity at present are pollution, environmental destruction and the rapid increase in the elderly and infirm. These problems cannot be solved by State intervention or market forces, but by a caring mentality.

Being constantly threatened in his adolescent-minded ego, man is under tension caused by an extra secretion of the emergency hormones and neurotransmitters, among these, testosterone.

152

Being irritating, the male hormone, testosterone, contributes to man's instant, impulsive and self-centred reasoning and behaviour, which damages his long-term interests, the interests of his species, those of other species and the planet as a whole. Man's mentality to-day is that of confrontation which is contrary to the basic interest of our social species, what is more, a species producing a growing number of welfare dependent people. The basic interest of our species is understanding, conciliation and cooperation which are spontaneous with a caring and sharing mentality.

It seems that testosterone hormones influence our moods and our mental activity by irritating the endocrinological mechanism of the brain's main gland, the hypothalamus. This irritation increases man's impatience, intolerance, aggression and violence. In fact, when for seasonal or artificially induced increases of the testosterones in man's body, there is a marked increase in crime, arsons, road accidents, accidents at work, poor decisions making, rape and battering of women, child abuse, litigations and a less efficient performance of students in their exams.

We are towards the end of a millenium. The end of a millenium and the beginning of a new one bring serious individual and collective tensions. We incline to give importance to rare events in history in order to increase our own importance by being part of these important events. Feeling more important, increases our pretensions which in turn increase our individual and social restlessness, agitation, racial, religious or ethnic persecutions, wars or ethnic cleansings.

The famous historian, Ferdinand Gregorovius, stressed: "It is indeed a remarkable historical phenomenon, that in periods of decadence some female figure generally rises into prominence."

Our present crisis is deeper than any other in history. It is the crisis of man's arrogant mind, its wishful beliefs and its pretentious ideologies. More and more man is faced with the failure of his beliefs and ideologies. This can be seen by the over-expansion of man's beliefs which, in fundamentalism and terrorism,are reaching their extremes, the prelude to explosion and their end.

Without his wishful beliefs and his pretentious

ideologies, man is lost. When man is lost, he leans on woman, placing his trust in her. Eliminating a great deal of his fears, this trust helps man to discover the notion of the future, a notion which could lead him to maturity. The supreme achievement of life, the very justification of an existence, is maturity. In any form of life, maturity implies fruitfulness and yielding on which the future of all life leans.

NECESSARY MEASURES

In our social species, economic wealth and the private property of this wealth can only be justified if they are in the interests of society. They can only be in social interest if they are manipulated by those in possession of a better developed humane brain, the brain which carries the needs for caring, loving, sharing and social interest.

Having a better developed humane and social brain, woman is more entitled to own the private property of economic wealth. The private property of economic wealth in the hands of man encourages his cult of individualism, his cult of individual autonomy, of selfishness, self-centredness, privacy, self-interest, isolation and loneliness, all of which are anti-social.

In order to enable economic wealth and its private property to be in the interest of the community, the legislator should introduce a law allowing the inheritance of economic wealth to pass through the female line.

We men are ready to graciously condescend and recognise that women are more socially minded, more community orientated and far superior to men in common sense reasoning, loving, caring, sharing and self-abnegation. But we tend to stop here. We never think to give women a chance to practice all these qualities. This would help woman to be herself, to use her wider way of reasoning in which the notion of the future is implicit. This would help woman in the education of her children and in helping her children to develop a more humane brain. This would help man to abandon his protracted adolescence and to reach a more civilised and a more humane life, a life of maturity.

Finding herself in a better economic condition, thus trusting herself more, woman would be in a better position to reduce the dangerous population explosion in the world. Only woman and only when she is allowed by better economic conditions to be her real self, can she limit the population growth. The females of most species carry an innate mechanism which controls the birth rate in tune with the environmental potential.

155

With a better economic situation, woman would be able to bring sexual selection to its natural order in which it is the female which initiates and rules her sexual activity and her conception.

One of the main characteristics of modern society is the steady increase in property crime. I am sure, that if the private property of economic wealth was used more in the social interest, than in man's inflated personal ego, shame would prevent a great deal of this crime. This crime would diminish even more if the judiciary system were in the hands of women.

It might even help woman to be more herself if instead of taking her husband's name in marriage, she kept her own. This could help man to reduce his sense of importance thereby helping him to reach maturity.

The children should also inherit their mother's name. After all, there is a significant biological reason for this. Every child has far more of its mother in its make up than of its father.

The mother's egg is a hundred thousand times bigger than the father's sperm and it is from her egg that the new life evolves. The egg is a complete cell, with its protoplasm, its mechanism for the production of proteins, its enzymes and its mitochondria, these power stations which provide energy for the cell's activities. Mitochondria, inherited only through the female, have their own independent genes. In fact, a great deal of these mitochondrial genes go back to the first Eves.

What is more, the mother's egg carries its specific organisation, its own characteristic metabolism and its own weakest part or organelle, its own "locus minoris resistantiae", all of which influence the personality and behaviour of the new creature.

During her pregnancy a mother's emotional experiences leave a lasting impact on her child's neuronal network. These emotional experiences influence the hormonal activities of the foetus which can predispose the offspring's mental life. It is a fact that particularly stressful pregnancies (during wars or revolutions), for example, produce an increased number of people with mental or even sexual deviations or disorders. The generation which tended towards rebelliousness and permissiveness in the Sixties were mainly those whose foetal developments took place during the Second World War.

During the nine months of her pregnancy the human mother transmits the main basic fears of our species to her unborn child. It is these basic fears which are deeply engraved in our memory and which frame the basic mental structures we all have in common as a species. It is these fears, transmitted to us when we were in our mother's uterus, which shape what C.G. Jung called "archetypes".

Without a mother's care and nurturing during the first months of its life, few babies would survive.

The father's contribution to new life is only half of his chromosomes.

Perhaps, it is in the name of these half chromosomes that the father contributes to the new life, that science, mainly dominated by men, has invented the myth of the predominance of the new god, the omnipotent and omnipresent gene, which is supposed to rule life. The followers of gene prepotency, however, avoid explaining that in order to become active a gene has to be activated by a cell and the cell's organization which are inherited from the mother's egg.

The difference between the genes of a chimpanzee and those of a man, seems to be less than two per cent. The difference between a chimpanzee and a man seems, therefore, to be due more to the difference between their original cells and to these cells' organisations and organelles, inherited from their mothers, than to the difference between their genes.

To-day's popular theory of the "selfish gene" could only have been invented and accepted by the selfish minds of men. Being detached from reality, man's selfish mind tends to see everything in its own image. A mother would have never invented the theory of the "selfish gene".

With these changes a great deal of stress and stress-related diseases and mental disorders, created by the ideology of patriarchy, would be reduced. Man's patriarchal mentality is stressful for man, woman and children: man has to perform a role imposed by his wishful ideology of patriarchy, woman and children have to perform their roles

157

in tune with the father's performance. That is why many observers of life imposed by the present culture consider it as a pathetic and comic theatre, pathetic for the performers and comic for the observers.

These changes would reduce one of the ugliest sides of life imposed by the present culture: reducing man's violence against women, children and nature. Becoming his real self, no longer pretending or performing the role of the ought to be wishful self, man would no longer need to prove his potency or his prepotency.

By law, a wife or a woman living with a man "more uxoris" should be entitled to a salary, either from her partner's employer, or from the community.

In February 1993, a British insurance company established that the average wife is worth about £ 349 a week for her work as cook, cleaner, laundress, shopper, dishwasher and various other domestic duties. If she also cares for a child then she should earn £457 a week. The survey established that even a wife with part-time employment still works an average of 59 hours a week at home and a wife in a full-time job often spends more hours on domestic activities than in the office or factory.

When any government presents its annual balance sheet, there is always one item missing: the contribution to the national economy of the domestic work of sisters, mothers, grandmothers, wives and mistresses.

The new culture would radically change the role of the economy in our lives.

Each of our brains has its own economic rationality. The economic rationality of the reptilian brain, which dominates when we live in fear or anxiety is quite different from the economic rationality of a mature or humane brain, the former representing crafty expediency, ruthless exploitation and instant gratification, the latter, a deeper and wider intelligence, caring and a strategy for the future.

Our present culture, dominated by the reptilian cult of individualism, has given competitive economy and its ruthless pursuit of material wealth, absolute priority in life. In fact, our present crisis is due to the fact that Western capitalism's utilatarianism, expediency, exploitation and scoring have penetrated into every aspect of our existence, from loving and courting, to marriage and friendship. This has killed the quality of life. All this has increased fears, anxieties and stress, which brings out the destructive reptilian legacy in us.

Economic material growth, profit and exploitation are our mind's obsessions because they appeal to our male ego and its sense of importance; they are considered progress or success.

Being an obsession, economic growth is contrary to nature and its basic tendency. Growth increases uncertainty, instability and complexity and these increase anxieties and fears. The main tendency in nature, the basic principle of life, is lesser instability, lesser complexity, lesser anxieties and fears.

Most of our present economic growth is governed not by our needs but by our desires which are insatiable.

As I said before, the main purpose of material and immaterial worlds is lesser restlessness and agitation, lesser instability. The supreme aim of the subatomic and the atomic worlds is to reach a ground rate, a lower energy state, a lesser uncertainty. We are made of these particles, but our mind leans on illusions above nature. The basic principle of our universe is the conservation of energy or the minimal use of it, the principle under permanent pressure in the world of the mind's ego and its insatiable desires.

Gravity, the main force in the universe, from subatomic particles to the galaxies, aims at lesser instability. Everything from subatomic particles to galaxies gravitates towards more stability. Only the human mind tries to break this law in the name of its wishful desires. As by its very nature a desire tends to expand, to result in greed, it ends in destabilising or destroying its environment and therefore itself.

In expanding our wishful desires, our mind prevents us from maturing. Continuous growth prevents maturity and the serenity of lesser instability.

Most of our economic growth is ruled, not by our biological or existential needs, but by our ego's desire and greed. This makes most of our economic growth unnecessary. Being unnecessary our economic growth is excessive which makes it disharmonising and damaging.

Economic activities inspired by needs are subject to the rule of diminishing returns until they reach a natural balance in an equilibrium in the needs' gratifications. Economic activities inspired by the mind's ego's desires are based on increasing returns: the more, the merrier.

When an individual belongs to a community he reduces his ego, his ego's fears and anxieties. Reducing fears and anxieties is the principal aim in life. Serving the community and its spirit, the economy's main purpose should therefore be to help its members reduce their fears and anxieties.

Our present economy and its growth merely increases the individual's fears and anxieties. The supreme purpose of a mature economy is not growth which increases precariousness but a better stability, a reduced uncertainty and precariousness.

Economic growth created in order to gratify the ego's desires, increases the ego's pretensions. An ego's pretensions increase the fear that these pretensions might not be fulfiled. It is in this fear, in fact, that we find the main source of the ugliness and low quality of Western life.

In our obsession for economic growth no-one ever thought to calculate the negative side-effects, or the unhealthy consequences of it. These negative side-effects of economic growth are: larceny, theft, car-stealing, murder, aggression, violence, alcohol abuse, drug-addiction, stress, stress-related diseases and mental disorders.

One of the most negative side-effects of the obsessive pursuit of economic growth is that parents who dedicate their lives to the economic improvement of their status or image abandon their children, or leave them in isolation with expensive electronic toys or games, which transforms them into obtuse infants for the rest of their lives. The damage caused by the behaviour of this obtuse human element can be far worse than the value of the increased wealth created by their parents.

The destabilising power of excessive economic wealth is best seen among the children of the rich, particularly when they inherit a great deal of money or

160

economic values from their parents. Often these young people rush to dissipate their inheritance in order to eliminate the fears and anxieties caused by living with it.

A rich person is not necessarily someone who has material wealth, but one who has moderate desires and limited pretensions. " The bigger a man's head, the worse his headache," goes a Persian proverb.

The obsession with economic growth can reach criminal proportions. In the last fifteen years governments, industry and trade have created and propagated consumerism, especially among the young, offering them all manner of credit which flatters their egos but which often hypothecates the rest of their lives.

Many political and religious leaders, along with the public at large, complain that moral values have collapsed, especially among the young and that there is a chronic increase in juvenile crime. But what kind of society can one expect when business, banking and trade bosses perceive annual salaries often amounting to several hundred thousand pounds for being able to create profits by playing with the vanities and pretensions of the young and naive. We can not expect to have moral values among the young when the religious leaders tolerate the exploitation of the young by the ruthless and greedy and when political leaders facilitate credit to the inexperienced young, calling it stimulation of demand.

Any increase in economic growth increases its above mentioned negative side effects. There is positive evidence particularly in the USA, that in the wealthy countries in the West the people are less mentally and physically healthy than they were fifty years ago. Lately, a new disorder is spreading in economically prosperous countries known as "TATT", (Tired All The Time), which is a form of the chronic and acute fatigue syndrome known as "Yuppie Flu", another disorder that spread with economic growth.

In our obsession for economic growth we not only fail to see its negative side effects, but, we don't realise that the cost of these negative side-effects are slowly but surely overtaking the value of the economic growth. Evidence of this is the increasing deficits and public debts of most of the countries so obsessed by economic growth.

This brings us to a paradox that only man's mind could have created: Western capitalism's pursuit of economic growth is basically the pursuit of insolvency or bankruptcy.

Anyone can verify this statement by comparing the amount spent by American federal and local governments on poverty programmes against the increase in the gross national production over the last fifty years, a poverty which was mainly created by the unscrupulous pursuit of economic wealth.

One could also add that a large portion of the value of economic growth goes against the cost of the national military forces so needed to protect national economic interests in the ruthless international competition for economic growth.

Increasing uncertainty and fears, economic growth inspired by wishful desires reduces our ability to plan the future. The greater the instability or uncertainty, the more instant is the way of reasoning and acting and the lesser is the notion of the future. In fact, in many countries economic growth is only realised on credit, at the expense of the future.

Carrying individual selfishness and self-interest, the pursuit of economic growth destroys the community and its spirit.

Increasing individual restlessness, the pursuit of economic growth contributes to the destruction of the community in another way as well. Restlessness creates mobility. In fact, in order to perpetuate itself, liberal capitalism glorifies and propagates the mobility of the labour force. Mobility implies loss of roots. People without roots become ruthless in their competition for material wealth.

Many are also attracted by mobility because it increases anxiety, an anxiety which we call excitement, amusement or fun. In this fun we seldom realise that our senses, perception and reasoning are restricted.

The other negative side of economic growth is that it is only calculated in quantitative material terms.

Another negative side-effect of the obsessive pursuit of economic growth is that it creates the greatest possible

162

misery: individual loneliness. We even consolidate and perpetuate the misery of loneliness by acquiring individual social and civil rights.

One could ask " Why are we so obsessed with the pursuit of unnecessary economic growth?"

The first answer to this question is because we are in a state of a mental disorder, we are in a state of intoxication, drugged by our pretentious ideologies and our wishful beliefs. We have the illusion that by increasing material wealth and its consumption, our intoxication will be justified.

The second answer to this question is that our obsession in the pursuit of growth in material wealth creates uncertainty, an uncertainty in which we find our addictive narcotic drug: excitement. Excitement helps us to become insensitive to reality and its boring rationality, keeping us out of touch with reality, thereby allowing the freedom of illusions and delusions.

The pathos of this is that, influenced by our reptilian legacy's cult of appearance, even when in despair, we often pretend we are happy in our restlessness and excitements. Contentment and serenity are unknown to the reptilian mentality.

In its expansion, Western capitalism created another ugly phenomenon in nature: consumerism, consumption of the unnecessary. Through clever advertising and ruthless marketing concentrated mainly on the ego's vanity, image, status, pretensions, or flattery, Western capitalism convinces people to develop and to increase their desires for more and more of the goods it produces in its growth.

The insatiableness of our desires and our greed is the major incentive of capitalism's expansion.

Consuming more than we need, we obviously work more than we need and often more than our organism can accept. This creates all kinds of stress related diseases and mental disorders. We are the only animal in nature able to create unnecessary stress.

What is the answer?

By becoming mature and serious we could eliminate our present obsession with the pursuit of economic growth.

In reducing this obsession we might realise that by starting to save, we could eliminate the pursuit of economic growth therefore many of the negative side-effects it creates.

We could start by saving the simplest thing to save: energy. We pay a lot from our economic growth on wasted energy, on the unnecessary or excessive use of it.

In our obsession with the idea of expansion, we are desperately searching for new sources of energy. Eliminating this obsession, mature intelligence knows that the richest source of energy is its saving.

What is more, saving reduces instability, uncertainty, fears and anxieties. Saving helps the consolidation of economy.

Machiavelli's motto " The end justifies means," the major pillar of our short-sighted present culture and which contributes a great deal to our economical and ecological crisis, will be derided by mature humanity and its culture. This motto will be derided by the mature culture because it inspires mentally unhealthy behaviour and an irrational wastage of unrenewable natural resources merely to achieve pretentious, capricious or futile ego-appealing desires. A mature culture's motto will be an ecologically and economically sound one consisting of the advise such as " adjust our aims to our means", to our limited natural and human resources.

A policy of tax incentives for industries, corporations, households and individuals that save energy and natural resources would help the cult of saving and the cult of maturity.

The difference between consumerism and saving is that the former belongs to immaturity, the latter to maturity. Immaturity implies growth and growth consumes resources. Maturity implies saving. Saving provides dividends. That is why maturity is fruitful. In nature plants and animals reach maturity when they stop growing and vice versa.

Life on credit creates inflation, the enemy of saving. Economic policies based on spending and inflation are policies which consolidate and perpetuate immaturity with its excessive selfishness and ruthless self-interest. An economic policy based on credit and inflation, eliminating the spirit of effort or sacrifice, prevents lasting relationships which kills any spirit of community, all in the name of an individual's here and now expediency.

In maturity the community's economy will be based on cooperation. In Western free market economy we have a strenuous and economically damaging situation in which capital and labour compete against each other, each aiming at reaching its own predominance, its own absolute power.

Only cooperation implying collaboration of the participants in the production can be economically advantageous as it creates an extra value. Cooperative output is superior to the amount of the individuals' inputs of the participants in the production.

This can best be seen in the field of scientific research.

Economic cooperation will be greatly facilitated by a new inheritance law establishing that private property can only be transmitted through the female line. By nature woman is more cooperative and more community orientated than man. As I said before, however, private property can only be justified if it is in the community's interest.

A differentiated fiscal system which facilitates cooperation could be of great assistance.

That cooperation is an efficient system can be seen from the fact that the most successful species in over nearly four billion years of life's evolution are those who live in community and cooperation, species working together. It is a fact that the cooperative community of a social species can perform far superior activities or tasks compared with the potential of isolated individuals in a community.

Economic cooperation in our species is only possible if and when we reach maturity, when our humane brain predominates.

Communism tried to replace ruthless and inhumane capitalism's competition with collectivisation. With our present mentality based on the cult of individualism and individual autonomy, however, collectivisation had to be imposed by force and intimidation, thus making it economically unproductive and humanely abhorrent.

The most important innovation in post-capitalism

should take place in the field of work and employment.

Dominated by capital's pursuit of profit, liberal capitalism considers work and the working force as its source of profit. Whenever profit can be higher or more easily realised by a machine, workers are replaced by it, thereby creating unemployment. Capitalism calls this replacement "rationalisation of production."

With an increase in the globalisation of world economy and coupled with the increase in international competition, this rationalisation of economic productivity is expanding rapidly. In some countries it has already reached obsessive proportions, when the reduction of the labour force becomes compulsory, when sacking people means rationalisation.

In its obsessive rationalisation, liberal capitalism does not realise that by increasing unemployment it increases the State's social assistance to the unemployed. This increase in the State's assistance has to be met by the tax-payer, which aggravates the capitalist's cost of production. What is more, by increasing unemployment, capitalism reduces the demand for goods which reduces both production and profits.

Basically the present world economic crisis is created by an obsessive rationalisation of industries in developed countries. These industrially advanced countries insist on creating world-wide free trade. This can only result in the rich becoming richer and the poor poorer. Above all, this free trade will create massive unemployment in countries of the second and third worlds. This free trade will fill the shops of under-developed countries with a variety of goods produced by rich countries, which the local people will not be able to buy. What is more, any talented person of under-developed countries who is able to contribute to the welfare of his country, will be bought and imported by one of the rich countries.

When unemployment, politically or socially sinks to dangerous levels, many governments reduce the official rate of interest so that cheaper credit improves productive investments, thereby reducing unemployment.

It is in the nature of politicians to act under pressure. It is also typical of acts made under pressure to be panicky and short-sighted. A sense of past and future disappear in panic.

Cheaper credits do not necessarily increase productive investments because there is no need for more production as unemployment and recession reduce the demand. Even in cases of new investment, industries prefer labour-saving technology to be introduced.

What is more, with our mentality becoming more and more orientated towards instant profit, any decrease in the cost of money increases not the productive but speculative investments which increase economic uncertainty and instability.

Some people insist that cheaper borrowing stimulates consumption thereby increasing the demand for goods. This increased demand, they claim, increases production which reduces unemployment. This reasoning fails to take into consideration that a lower interest rate reduces the value of savings. This lessens interest in saving thus reducing people's labouriousness, their incentives to work. In fact, a lasting policy of low interest rates can produce indolence, indifference, apathy and absenteeism.

Any increase in unemployment aggravates the mental and physical health of the unemployed, thereby increasing the cost of the community's health service. Shaken in their essence and in the efficiency of their immune systems, unemployed people become open to all kinds of opportunistic infections and depression. Those who remain employed during an era of high unemployment can also become susceptible to diseases and mental disorders, due to fear of joining the unemployed. Secondly, when companies become obsessed with reducing the cost of production by the reduction of the working people, the remaining workers are often forced to work harder and longer hours in order to cope with the work which was done by those who were sacked. This extra fatigue can be dangerous for their mental and physical health which also aggravates the cost of the community's health service.

In search of economic growth, profit and scoring, the globalisation of world economy and trade increases international competition which means replacing the working force with science and technology more and more. This increases unemployment which can be economically, socially and politically dangerous.

What is the solution?

First of all, the economy must descend from its imperial dominating and dictatorial position to its natural place in the community, to serve the community. Only the community and belonging to it can reduce our individual existential fears and anxieties. Western capitalism with its cool, detached, reptilian-minded free market, which by now is the supreme regulator of even our most intimate relations and which considers itself the great victor in ideological wars with other ideologies, has to come down from its pretentious pedestal. It must wake up to reality and realise what kind of humanity it has shaped and what horror of ecological and moral misery it has contributed to. By building itself on the cult of individualism and individual autonomy, liberal capitalism has destroyed the protective family and community, leaving the individual in his agonising isolations, in which his fears reach paranoiac proportions.

Many experts insist that high unemployment contributes to the disintegration of our society, our community and our family.

Would it not be more accurate to stress that the destruction of society, the community and our family was realised by the free market economy which creates uncaring people and unemployment in the first place.

Instead of being guided by ego pleasing material profit, the new post-capitalist economy should be based on the principle "work for all". Being a need of the humane brain, work must be made available for anyone in need of it. Without work, those in need of it easily slip back into their reptilian existence. In fact, the community's real wealth would be the availability of work and its supreme aspiration the increase of this availability. The values of labour and its productivity should be based on contributions to the spirit and the welfare of the community and above all on peoples' contribution in enabling the community to reduce the fears and anxieties of its members. In order to achieve this more easily, labour will not be considered a commodity, sold and bought on a free market, but an offer to participate, to belong, or, to be employed in the communal effort in building a happier, safer and a more serene community.

As I stressed, the availability of work in a community is its true wealth. The fair redistribution of this wealth among the members of the community should be the main policy of the post-capitalist community. Being fair, this policy will help in the consolidation and perpetuation of the community's spirit. The fair redistribution of available work, practiced by its sharing, will consolidate and perpetuate the reassuring feeling of belonging and solidarity, both of which help mature reasoning and mature rationality.

With the help of more mature professional organisations, the available work sharing could easily be realised through job-sharing or part-time work. These more mature professional organisations will look upon the present reptilian reasoning and rationality and its short-sighted trade unions with derision.

Sharing creates fairness and fairness is the best stimulus of an economically productive cooperation.

The community's fiscal and credit policies must facilitate companies which practice job-sharing or part-time work, In fact, each company's annual balance sheet should show an evaluation of the company's contribution to the community's interest. This evaluation of the company's contribution to the community's interest should be taken into consideration in fixing the level of the company's taxation.

Pension funds, these important sources of investment capital which manipulate people's savings, could be a major factor in the post-capitalist economy based on the cult of work. These investments of pension funds could also contribute a great deal to lessen the fears and anxieties of their members if they are made in companies helping to reduce unemployment which can bring the social unrest so feared by pensioners or by those who invest in their retirement.

The lives of life insurance companies' clients would be more serene if these companies invested their capital into firms which create a better social existence and climate.

To those who prefer stimulating uncertainty to the serenity of certainty and who will be the first to call my idea of the future "Utopia", I have one simple answer. We have reached a point in which we have no choice: either we share work, or we share unemployment, the fear of unemployment, violence, crime, vulgarity, suicide and a chain of new opportunistic diseases, besides an increase in stress-related mental disorders. In fact, I would like to emphasise that we might soon face vast epidemics of certain opportunistic diseases if we continue to increase stress and frustrations. For millions of years we have carried a variety of viruses in our bodies, kept dormant by our immune defences. If we continue to lower the efficiency of our immune system we could well reach a point in which these dangerous viruses could spring to life.

In many countries there is a proverb inspired by experience and wisdom: " a burden shared is a burden halved." An old Italian proverb even considers a catastrophe less catastrophic if it is shared.

By greatly reducing our existential fears and anxieties, sharing work and belonging to a protective and fair community, our humane brain's need for caring, loving, helping, nursing and nurturing will come into prominence. Due to the serious problem of a continuous increase in the elderly and disabled population, which is often totally dependent on the community, the need for caring is vital. We must noticeably increase the efficiency of our activities and work, particularly in the West, in order to be able to cope with the increasing elderly and disabled population on one side and the decreasing number of young and able on the other. The most powerful incentive to a keener efficiency of both work and activities is caring. Only caring can save the community-dependent people. Without caring we will soon start, through the mounting reduction of economic support , eliminating all the dependents. Even in our culture, caring voluntary and benevolent work is highly efficient and beneficiary.

To those who might consider my ideas unpractical, I advise them to try and visualise the alternative, which can only be total economic collapse due to the increasing cost of social and health services.

In order to be able to share the available work of a

community better, the working week should be reduced by an United Nations Charter to 25 hours. International economic sanctions should be applied against the countries and communities which do not accept or conform to the Charter. The globalisation of world economy has globalised the problem of unemployment.

Reducing the working hours will allow more time to dedicate to caring, loving, understanding, tolerating, more time to use our humane brain, more time for voluntary work. Using our mature brain we will realise that our present working time and over-time is laughable because it is unnecessary. Being unnecessary it is excessive and being excessive it destroys our living habitat by inhibiting or preventing its renewability.

A reduction in working hours will give us time to develop and to cultivate the curiosity so essential for a keener participation in life and in its enjoyment. Our present working hours limit our interest in a wider life and in others, mainly because we are so exhausted and stressed.

Reduced working hours will enable women to have more time with the family and the community. The present working week does not suit a women's nature because it was invented and perpetuated by man's reptilian mentality which has little family or community sense of responsibility.

More and more women are working to-day many of them employed in the service industry in which sharing available work could easily be arranged. Being more mature than men and less ego-minded, the sharing of work and cooperation are more in women's nature.

Freer economic independence, mainly due to the inheritance of economic wealth through the female line, plus shorter working hours for employed women will all help the new family, a family concentrated around the mother, around the "mater familias", a family more suited to nature and its laws. Dedicating more time, more loving and caring to their children, mothers will be able to help their children to develop superior brains, to become part of a more serious, more mature and a more caring humanity.

Many people claim that there is a crisis in family values. As I said before, this crisis started some 10.000

171

years ago when man started assuming the artificial role of the dominant patriarchal "pater familias", when he started coercing women and children to adapt themselves to his wishful belief of the predominant male.

Many so-called experts insist that the increase in juvenile crime is due to the fact that more and more children grow up in families without a father. This is true in present male culture. In fact, many children's rebellious behaviour and attitudes are against the male culture and values, imposed by man by force, by force lacking authority or respect.

Religious and political leaders insist that the only solution to the present crisis of values is to go back to the traditional lost values. They do not realise that the traditional values were wrong even in the past, that by now most of them are fossils. The sooner men realise that their moral and religious values are dead or dying, the sooner they will mature. The best cure of a mental disorder and the culture based on men's wishful beliefs and ideologies is a mental disorder, is to become aware of it. Once we become aware of our mental disorder, we become cured.

In post-capitalism, retirement will be gradual, starting at the age of 55 years. With each subsequent year working hours will slowly be reduced.

The working hours of the young will start slowly, increasing gradually with age.

This will help intergeneration relationships and solidarity, so important in building the cult of the community.

With a more mature life, unemployment benefits will become an irrational practice of the past. Irrational because these benefits were financing inactivity and State dependence which create infantile obtuseness, a major source of crime and vandalism. What is more, financing inactivity reduces the working enthusiasm of those employed who are taxed in order to pay the unemployment benefits.

University students will be granted scholarships from the community on the condition that they spend the same amount of years spent at universities in community's social services, exercising their acquired profession at a lower salary a, fair equality of opportunity.

In order to run its economy and its social life more efficiently and fairly, a community should not go beyond the municipal level. The State, a group of States and the United Nations will facilitate and protect the municipalisation of world economy. The globalisation of the world economy has brought into evidence the need for world cooperation, especially in view of the population explosion and the vast migration of starving people towards richer countries.

In order to be able to cooperate economically and politically on a global level, we need small communities because these create spirit and the ability to cooperate without which we can not cooperate on a global level.

With the more mature mentality, which is cooperative by nature, there will be no competition between the municipalities.

As I stressed before, many people insist that competition is in the nature of the human male. Again I repeat that this is true but only on a primitive level, when we are dominated by our primitive reptilian brain. In maturity we acquire a different nature which is cooperative in its essence. Maturity is cooperative because it is wise, because it reasons in a wider and a deeper way, in which the future and the quality of life are major considerations.

In fact, cooperation is the basic principle of existence. An atom would never exist without the cooperation of its sub-atomic particles, a molecule would not be able to exist without the cooperation of its atoms, an element could not be formed without the cooperation of its molecules. Without the universal principle of cooperation we would never have had a multicellular organism because we would not have had differentiation of cells and the morphogenesis which form the multicellular organism.

What is also important is that contrary to competition which cultivates dangerous and damaging secrecy, cooperation implies openness, communications and consultation, essential in order to reduce the wastage of energy and resources.

What is more, by eliminating tense and stressful

173

individual antagonism and competition, cooperation contributes to the quality of production and its products which increases a sense of solidity or trust and reduces the atmosphere of uncertainty and instability .

With our present culture and values, we never take into consideration the quality of life. Quantitative measurements appeal more to the primitive man and to his obsession to appear bigger.

Lesser salaries or wages, received from lesser working hours will be compensated by better public services. Improved public services reduce the cost of living.

Better public education reduces the need for private education or tuition. In order to provide their children with private education or tuition, many parents have to work long over-time hours to earn the necessary extra money.

More efficient public transport would reduce the need for so many private cars and the many working hours necessary to buy and service a car. Eliminating a lot of private cars would also reduce air pollution and the cost caused by fighting it or fighting the consequences of it. Reducing private cars would also reduce the depressing ugliness of our streets packed with parked monsters.

The new culture will improve the public health service by reducing the abuse of it and by replacing the morally corrupt market mentality with a more mature cooperation at all levels.

Above all, the new culture will lower the cost of the public health service because it will eliminate a great deal of stress, thus reducing stress related diseases and mental disorders. By reducing working hours, post-capitalism will eliminate physical fatigue, another contributor to stress and a high cause of bad accidents at work.

Creating more free-time, post-capitalism will make time for voluntary help with the public health service which will both improve the service and reduce its cost. With our present culture and values the cost of health services world-wide is financed by public borrowing. This leads to bankruptcy.

Better public services will contribute to the improvement of the community's global economic performance as it will increase the efficiency of agricultural and manufacturing industries as well as that of trade.

Lesser wages perceived for lesser working hours will be compensated by a greatly improved quality of life and a better quality of goods, all of which contributes to solidity, respect and dignity, essential pillars of the quality of life. In fact, in the community's annual economic performance report, the quantitatively calculated gross domestic production should be accompanied by a report stating the community's qualitative achievements.

Loss of economic growth in the community caused by the reduction of working hours will be compensated by a saving in the cost of the negative side-effects of economic growth. Most people who are obsessed with the present Western style capitalism do not realise that they have reached a paradox. After a certain number of working hours, any further economic activity can only bring negative results, the cost of which is higher than its material benefices.

Post-capitalist economy will give absolute priority to the services, not only because of their contribution to human dignity which helps human humaneness or because of their contribution to the quality of the production, the quality of life and the quality of the habitat, but because services can easily practice job-sharing, so essential to the policy of full employment.

What is more, reduced salaries, compensated for by the improved public services, can help employment in other industries or trade.

Without a more mature economy ruled by a more humane brain and without an economy which gives greater importance to public services, we will soon have a serious problem with the continuous increase in old, disabled or community dependent people.

The new culture will give special importance to the service of prevention of negative events for two reasons. Firstly, this service will be able to employ a great deal of people. Secondly, preventing diseases and mental disorders, accidents and invalidness, crime and violence, vandalism and social disorder, pollution and environmental damage, alcoholism and drug addiction, can all save a great deal of resource:. The cost of the service of preventions will be far

175

inferior to the cost of the negative events that could happen had they not been prevented.

Our present culture and mentality have never given due importance to the idea of prevention because it does not suit our immature and instant way of thinking.

The concept of prevention belongs to a more mature brain, able to reason with a notion of the future, with the idea of what might happen beyond the here and now.

The prevention of negative events is somehow less glamourous and less ego-appealing than the expensive but often futile research for their cures.

The obsession with the pursuit of reduction in the cost of production, through a reduction in the working forces, is even invading the service industry.

Replacing the human factor in service with automatic machines or robots, alienates individuals from each other, contributing to obtuseness and the moroseness of loneliness.

The automatization of the services can even damage the community's economy in material terms. For example, with the introduction of automatic self-service petrol stations some 60.000 assistants have been made redundant. Keeping them employed would only have raised the price of petrol about one percent. Now, unemployed, these sacked assistants have to be helped by the community's taxes, some of whom do not even use gas stations. What is even more paradoxical is the cost of automatic machines and their maintenance has to be covered by raising the price of petrol higher.

The service industry has always been looked down on by other industries, particularly the manufacturing industry. This is mainly due to our culture's obsession with the mind's ego and its sense of importance. The manufacturing industry has always flattered the male ego, man's masculinity; it was his territory, his source of dominance.

With the computerisation of the manufacturing industry, just as easily manipulated by women, man has been shaken in his very essence, in his ego inspired identity.

One of the main reasons for the fall of communist

economy was the obsession and glorification of the manufacturing industry at the expense of the services.

An economy based on rationalisation of this industry will soon need less and less people. Some experts are calculating that in the next century only two percent of the present number of workers employed in manufacturing will be needed to produce the same amount of goods produced today.

On the other hand, employment in the service industry continues to increase. In most industrially developed countries, employment in the services has increased over the past 40 years from under 40% to around 70% of the working population.

The service industry will have difficulty in excessive replacement of humans by machines, because after a certain limit an excessively mechanised service becomes a caricature of the service thereby making it less competitive with more human and humane services.

Here it could be suggested that the reduction of working hours will increase free time. Free time can result in boredom and boredom is often a serious source of all manners of negative, expensive and unhealthy attitudes and behaviour.

The tragic paradox of our culture which cultivates man's ego can be found in the phenomenon of boredom. An inflated ego is flattered by free time and leisure and strives for as much as possible. But, we pay for it. Freedom carries fears. What is more, in free time we have the impression that reality is staring at us with its deriding smile, which is even more frightening.

These fears create boredom. Boredom in essence consists of an inflated ego's fears. In fact, the level of the adrenalin in the blood of a bored person is far higher than in those who are content.

In order to placate his boredom, a bored person tries to escape from deriding reality. This escape can be positively damaging and what is more, like any other escape, the bored person's escape perpetuates or increases his original fears. Some people try to escape into obesity, some into alcoholism or drug-addiction, some in crime or violence, some in joy-riding or vandalism.

Some inflated or infatuated egos face reality with apathy, hopelessness or depression. It is in these states that our mind often develops hallucinations or delusions.

Some inflated or infatuated egos even pray to their divinities to gratify their wishful pretensions.

Some of these egos try to find solace in complaining. In the mind of a bored person, complaining gives the impression of increasing his importance. Complaining, however, transforms the bored into the boring, which isolates him even more.

Students are bored by subjects that do not flatter their egos, or by subjects that offend their inflated egos because they do not understand them. This kind of boredom usually results in aggression against the fragile or elderly, into mugging, hooliganism or vandalism.

That boredom is mainly related to the male inflated ego can be best seen from the fact that it reaches its maximum levels in male adolescence when the ego and its self-centredness reach their peak.

The bad news for egomaniacs who are easily bored is that creating tension, boredom reduces the efficiency of our immune defences, rendering us susceptible to infections. Boredom also increases neurological and gastro-intestinal disorders, as well as cardiovascular diseases. Increasing tension, boredom can cause sleeplessness, intolerance, agitation, restlessness, rushing and risky adventurousness.

Boredom increases absenteeism from work and desertion from duties. It also makes us accident prone.

Boredom is often a cause of suicide. Most suicides, in fact, take place on a Sunday when added leisure can become intolerable.

Between the two World Wars, Hungary was at the top of the international suicide list. A Hungarian composer discovered that most suicides took place on a Sunday, which inspired him to compose a famous tango "Sad Sunday". In 1951, he committed suicide on a Sunday, probably listening to his own music.

Being more mature and less egomaniacal, women are less bored than men, although women with the Athena syndrome can be as bored as men, even "bored to death".

Eliminating the inflated ego by becoming more mature, man could easily achieve the opposite of boredom, the joyfulness and contentment of those who use their leisure in activities which gratify the humane brain's needs.

Another frequent inflated ego's escape from boredom is entertainment. Entertainments please the ego's sense of importance. But, what is even more significant, entertainments involve excitements, enabling the inflated ego to become insensitive to offending or threatening reality.

Many people try to assert their ego, shaken by boredom, by creating fictional art or literature, or by escaping into philosophising. Many of these writers or philosophers, who deserted reality and escaped into fantasy try to illuminate us about the meaning of real life, about the meaning of its meaning. And what is even more ridiculous, the mediocrity and above all pseudo-intellectuals, applaud them, especially when they do not understand them or grasp their meanings.

With the mature mentality in which our ego disappears and in which our humane brain comes into prominence, free time also vanishes. As I said before, in maturity, free time is filled with activities inspired by the humane brain's needs, such as loving, caring, helping those in need, nursing, nurturing, building the community, friendship, solidarity and relationships.

The lower individual, family and community's income, due to post-capitalism's reduced working hours, will find compensation in a significant amount of saving on entertainments. Eliminating the inflated and pretentious ego, the mature mentality will not need to be entertained or excited any longer, but will be fully involved in real life, in true contentment. A content or happy person has no need or desire for excitement or adventure.

Reducing the obsession with economic growth, the mature economy's reduced working hours will not only eliminate a great deal of unhealthy side-effects of this obsession, but it will help to reach better contentment and deeper happiness.

The level of the consumption of tranquillisers and sleeping pills by people or countries obsessed with the present capitalism's pursuit of economic growth is clear evidence that material prosperity does not bring contentment or happiness. There is a certain justice in Western countries' discontent or unhappiness with their material prosperity because a great deal of this prosperity has been realised by the ruthless exploitation of the rest of the world, some of which lives on total misery and poverty.

Free time will help domestic economy. It will contribute to the saving on repairs as far as the house and house goods are concerned. A domestic economy creates domesticity and homeliness with their calming and protective influences.

The mature policy to build the economy on the employment of the employable implies a less obsessive mechanisation of industries.

In its expansion, obsession with the mechanisation of industries has reached a serious mental disorder, a comic and tragic madness. Instead of being served by modern technology, it is us who serves a variety of machines. What is more, we serve the accelerated rhythm of modern technology, adapting our biological clock to a mechanical clock. This adaptation is, in fact, the major source of stress and stress related diseases and disorders of modern man.

The pathetic and comic automatization and mechanisation of modern man, so well depicted by Chaplin's satires, has dehumanised him.

In fact, it was the dehumanised reptilian brain which started creating the automatic mechanised self-services as they appeal to its individual isolation and autonomy.

The post-capitalist community should introduce a compulsory community's service, for at least a year, for those between the ages of 16 and 25.

This community service would offer training courses from plumbing to electricity, from repairing durable domestic goods to carpentry, from house painting to building. Less and less people can afford to pay for these repairs.

Learning these trades or skills would help the young to help themselves and to help each other, exchanging their skills and services. Being able to help oneself and others reduces much anxiety and panic when something goes wrong. Exchanging skills and services reduces the cost of living.

The compulsory community services would also be of a major importance in helping the old, invalid or helpless population. In order to be able to cope and help with the increasing community-dependent population and old-age pensioners, the government is forced to borrow more and more which is not economically, socially or politically wise or healthy. Before the First World War there were less than 1 million old pensioners, in the United Kingdom, costing the State £12.3 million a year. In 1950, the relative figures were: 4 million and £4.5 billion at today's prices; presently the figures are: 10 million and £26 billion.

But, what is much more important, this service could reduce old people's fears and anxieties, helping them to reach maturity and serenity. This would encourage them to integrate into the community. Fears and anxieties keep people inside reptilian selfishness and self-centredness, particularly the elderly which often alienates them from the rest of the community.

Learning and practicing a trade or a skill and above all practicing it for humane reasons, gives young people a more optimistic outlook on life and reasoning.

This compulsory community service would also help the young to develop team-spirit, a preventive and curative therapy against gang-spirit. The difference is that the former is cooperative in its essence, providing an extra value, a value which is superior to the sum of individual efforts put by each member of the team. In fact, it is in this cooperative team's extra value that we find the essence of real quality.

A team is like an orchestra which provides harmony from individual musicians playing a variety of instruments. A gang creates a cacophony in which each member tries to compete and out play each other on the same instrument.

Reducing fears and anxieties, togetherness, sociality and cooperation, so essential in a team, transforms team-work into a joyful, pleasurable or playful activity. This can help the young, who have never experienced joyful play, to discover it. It can also help them realise that individual excessive selfishness and exaggerated self-interest are

181

eliminated from play.

Team activities imply dialogue among team members. Reducing individual excesses through compromise, dialogue helps in saving resources and energy.

JUSTICE

Our immature culture is best reflected in present day justice.

Our justice is more concentrated on the persecution or punishment of sinners and criminals than in their redemption or salvation. Our "eye for an eye" justice is in tune with the reptilian legacy. This cruel reptilian logic insists that an injury must be compensated by inflicting the same injury in order to reduce the injurer's advantage in the competitive reptilian world.

Justice can only operate if people are aware of the difference between wrong and right. In our present culture most people live in an infant reptilian mentality, incapable of knowing the difference.

Concentrating more on punishment than on redemption, our present justice merely helps to create criminals. Punishment aims at bringing the wrong-doer to obedience. Reducing the wrong-doer to obedience, the judge reduces the wrong-doer to an even more obtuse infant mentality, in which wrong and right, good and evil do not exist. What is more, the fear of punishment by present day justice brings people's reptilian legacies into prominence.

Our justice is symbolised by a blind-folded woman which is supposed to represent impartiality.

A blind-folded person is an invalid. An invalid's main fear is to make a wrong decision, to commit an error. Nothing makes people more accident prone than the fear of it. Error in justice is an enormous error, it is injustice. This fear of justice's injustice encourages many people to provoke or to break the order defended by our justice.

Man's justice can never inspire general respect because it is not based on authority but on power and power carries aggression and coercion.

Christianity invented a wishful belief that suffering can redeem or rehabilitate a sinner or a criminal. This belief inspired torture, dehumanisation or unhealthy and claustrophobic confinement and prison.

Dehumanising humans, our prisons create

dehumanised reptilians. On the level of the reptilian mentality there is no redemption, but just a selfish and instant expediency guided by a primitive or crude utilitarianism.

What is more, as I said before, religious or political leaders have never understood that dehumanisation and affliction eliminate suffering. When in the reptilian level of existence even sensitivity and pain are greatly reduced.

That the reptilian legacy comes into prominence in our dehumanising prisons can be seen from the fact that the cult of aggression and violence and the cult of individual ruthless competition for rank or status are in evidence.

But, what is the silliest of our present system of justice, so obsessed with the punishment of the wrong-doer, is that it prevents the wrong-doer from repairing the damage he has done.

Having a slower development of the network of the mature brain, in our present male dominated culture, boys tend to remain in their infant mentality or adolescence longer than girls. Perhaps this is why more men than women commit crime and violence.

Many male scientists try to explain that breaking the law and order is in human nature, in our genes. Some of these scientists even accuse the victims of crime and violence of having provoked it either by their negligence or by their behaviour.

Car or house owners are accused of not having taken the necessary precautions, thereby encouraging criminals to steal. Women, too, are sometimes accused of dressing provocatively, thereby inducing the crime of rape.

This continuous increase in crime and violence indicates that if we do not start maturing, if we do not stop playing the game of wishful existence, if we do not adopt the new more realistic culture, we will soon be over-ruled by an even more primitive and ruthless infant mentality.

Evidence to prove my theory that most criminals are in a state of infant mental backwardness caused by underdevelopment of their superior brain, is the fact that most of them have a limited use of speech and vocabulary. This is because speech is mainly ruled by the emotions ruled

184

by the well developed limbic brain. When criminals have to communicate, they usually do it by gestures or body signs, which is of a reptilian origin. Even a normal person with a well developed organisation of the limbic brain and who is usually articulate in his speech, when in a primitive state of existence, induced either by strong fear, or panic, can become inarticulate and start to communicate with gesticulations.

In order to be more in tune with the humane humanity, justice should be maternal. This implies caring, loving, understanding, pity and sympathy.

In post-capitalism the judges should be selected from the most mature and most humane human element. Coupled with teachers, they ought to be in the highest bracket of salaries in the community. Our present culture is ridiculous where a pop-singer, a boxer, or a footballer earn a hundred times more than a judge.

The new culture's more humane judge will replace the paternalistic power of to-day's judge with a maternal authority, an authority implying respect because of its wider reasoning, because of its competence and because of its humaneness.

The supreme aim of the paternal judge is to reduce the criminal to obedience, to perpetuate infancy. The supreme aim of the maternal judge is to raise the infant to maturity. In maturity there is no crime or violence because it implies selflessness, fruitfulness, caring and giving.

Carrying humaneness, maternal authority inspires a sense of shame, the best deterrent against wrong-doing and the best stimulant for repairing the wrong-doing or encouraging doing good.

A sense of shame belongs to the humane brain; it does not exist on the level of the infant reptilian brain.

A sense of shame is preceded by an awareness of wrong, which, in essence, consists of an excessive self-interest or an immature selfishness, all parts of the reptilian existence.

When reduced to our reptilian existence by strong fears, we all reason and behave in a self-centred way which goes against the interests of others or against the community

185

as a whole. Most criminals in all fields of life feel unashamed while under the influence of their infant mentality.

The gradual decrease of a sense of shame in our present culture is best seen in our politicians, a clear sign of progressive degeneration towards an uncivilised society. More and more people even consider it degrading to be ashamed.

By escaping from a sense of shame, one is able to continue persevering in error or in wrong-doing, in this way causing damage to others and often to oneself, in order to save one's face, a legacy from the reptilian obsession with its image and appearance.

Avoiding a sense of shame or penitence for our errors or wrong-doing, can have serious consequences. Firstly it can be accident prone; secondly, people who avoid a sense of shame or penitence often try instead to punish themselves with physical harm, sometimes even serious self-mutilation.

Self destruction is on the increase which implies that there are more and more people who prefer to persevere in error rather than mend their ways.

The Christian religion invented Original Sin in order to create a permanent feeling of guilt and penitence, hoping in this way to reduce an individual's excessive self-interest. What the Christians did not realise was that by inventing a fearful God who demanded absolute obedience, it reduced people to the infant reptilian mentality, which is unable to feel penitence. An individual with an infant reptilian mentality cannot repent because he operates with an instant expediency guided by total self-interest.

When the Church demands penance we witness a comic performance of obedience, a performance in tune with reptilian ritualistic tendencies.

Instead of always sending criminals to prison where they usually acquire an even deeper criminal mentality, the maternal judge should place them into carefully chosen teams to work with the community performing public services.

Team work can be excellent therapy for criminals because most of them are in a state of retarded infancy.

Team-work can often become fun, a playful activity.

Many criminals acquired their retarded mental state because in infancy they seldom played with other children, which isolated them into a frightening obtuse loneliness. They never had the chance to develop sociality, togetherness, cuddling or contact with others. In fact, like true cold-blooded reptilians, most criminals fear intimacy or physical contact and often react violently even to an accidental body touch. Team-work can create a convivial atmosphere or a kind of social grooming and bondage which helps to reduce an individual's existential fears, thus reducing his selfishness and self-centredness.

Relating us to reality and to others, team-work gives the feeling of participation, of belonging, thus reducing the individual's fears, which helps the development and use of the superior brains.

With more and more children to-day playing video-games by themselves, or miles away listening to their own personal walkmans, it is easy to forecast a big increase in crime and violence.

Being more maternal and more mature than men, women should be more in prominence in the administration of justice. In the present culture, public service is considered a career for a man, in which his self-interest and ego-ruled status are predominant. For a woman, working for a public service is a dedication. In fact, for a woman any activity is usually a dedication because it is in her nature to put her innate caring and loving willingly into whatever she does. The best evidence of this is that women in public services are far less corruptible and far more difficult to bribe than men.

In the Cappella degli Serovegni in Padua, Giotto, in his subtle geniality, depicted his figure of justice as a serene benevolent and magnanimous mother, with her wide-open eyes, looking with maternal love at a group of people standing on her palm. Next to this picture, Giotto depicted the figure of injustice represented by an arrogant, aggressive looking self-righteous man. Giotto must have known that man's justice, inspired by his wishful belief was the very essence of injustice. Wishful beliefs have to be forced on reality which implies destroying reality, a crime and violence against it. Giotto knew that believer's self-rightousness is the source of injustice. Creating fear and resentment, injustice prevents us reaching maturity and civility.

To those who insist that man is the natural leader, I answer that wars, revolutions, persecutions, tortures, prisons, concentration camps, crime and violence and deterioration of the living habitat, are all the results of man's leadership.

To those who consider my ideas regarding justice as ridiculous I answer that persevering with the present culture means a regular increase in economic, political, social and environmental deteriorations.

That the present culture is expanding towards more chaos can be seen by the following figures. In 1946, in England and Wales there were 347 murders, 251 rapes, 921 robberies.Twenty years later there were 364 murders, 644 rapes and 4.474 robberies. In 1991 there were 725 murders, 4.045 rapes and 45.323 robberies. This rate of increase in crimes far exceeds the increase in population in England and Wales. The same trend can be found in all Western countries where reliable statistics are available.

That our culture is expanding towards a culture of crime and violence can also be deduced by the fact that people are more and more interested and excited by books, plays, films and media reportage dealing with crime and violence.

Increasing uncooperative and sometimes even hostile public attitude towards the police in their fight against crime and violence, is a serious sign of our degeneration into chaos.

To those who merely sigh nostalgically for the "good old days", I would like to point out that it was our so called glorious past which was the breeding ground for the present and for the disasters that the future promises.

The economic independence of women in the post-capitalist society will allow them to change many of the present laws and religious or moral norms which were created and enforced by men when women were denigrated, debased, in fact, when they were under total dominance of men. Bringing the positive laws and religious and moral norms of the present culture to more realistic and more natural levels, a great deal of the expensive justice administration will disappear. Natural laws do not need justice to enforce them. In fact, most of our present culture's justice is against natural justice; that is why our justice has to be coercive.

Man's mind 's wishfulness has to be imposed on reality which implies a wastage of human and natural resources.

One important law must be changed to the level of natural law, which would help the problem of over-population: the law dealing with the reproductive control. Allowing only woman to have the control of her reproduction would mean simply accepting the validity of the natural law.

The law dealing with pornography will also disappear. In maturity man becomes maternal. Maternal man does not need pornography to prove to himself his dominance over women.

CONTRIBUTOCRACY

Since man escaped from reality into the world of his mind, he became guided by abstract theories, dogmas or principles. These were usually created and based on the wishful beliefs or ideologies of those in power. Physical might became God's given right.

Western style democracy is nothing but a certain number of theories based on the wishful desires of those in power, power they obtain and keep through a Darwinian kind of free individual reptilian competition.

The cult of liberal individualism and of individual autonomy played a major part in destroying the feudal world, a world based on the wishful beliefs of those in power. The feudal system was replaced by middle-class democracy, created around wishful beliefs all in the interest of an individual's selfishness and selfish expediency which bourgeois philosophy calls pragmatism.

Western democracy glorifies itself, a clear sign that it is wishful. We only glorify wishful beliefs. We are the only animal capable of self-deception.

Like any other wishful belief, democracy produced absurdities when translated and enforced upon reality.

Western democracy leans on its sacrosanct cults, that of individualism and that of individual freedom and independence.

As I said before, the cults of individualism, individual freedom and autonomy, isolate an individual and a lonely individual is afraid.

In fear our reasoning is mainly ruled by our primitive reptilian brain. In reality, Western style democracy returns us to our primitive state of existence. In this primitive state of existence there is no individual freedom and individual autonomy. Our individual free choice, of which we are so proud, is nothing but an escape from an "or" because it inspires more fear than an "either".

What is more, in this primitive state of existence we are easily impressed, thus seduced, by pompous demagogy and by magic and illusions, which negate individual freedom and autonomy. On television, for example, we see how the success of a political leader can depend on his appearance or image, very much in tune with our reptilian legacy.

We are easily seduced by banners carrying slogans such as "freedom of thought', "consensus", "open society", "popular representation", "popular sovereignty", "equality of opportunity", "the pursuit of happiness", "all men are created equal", "rule of the people".

But if analysed these slogans, if we saw them caricatured by reality, we would realise their emptiness.

By separating an individual from his protective community in the name of individual freedom and autonomy, Western style democracy created individual restlessness and agitation, both sources of aggression and conquest. Fear created by individual isolation and loneliness returns us to our primitive mentality, the mentality of territoriality and possession.

Restlessness, agitation, aggression and conquest, provided and perpetuated by Western democracies, enabled Western Europe to subjugate the rest of the world, creating empires and imperial economy consisting of the ruthless exploitation of the human and natural resources of their colonies. This policy of exploitation goes on even now under the euphemistic term of technical and financial aid to underdeveloped countries.

The ruthless exploiting nature of Western culture can also be seen in the fact that its scientific discoveries were used more for aggressive purposes than for peaceful ones. The Chinese played with their explosive powder for centuries using it mainly for their pyrotechnical spectacles. When Western Europe discovered it, they transformed it into gun-powder.

Most Western Europeans are even proud of their imperial pasts and of having used their scientific and technological inventions for destructive purposes.

Western culture's social sciences and even biology and its evolution were invented by the mentality of isolated and lonely Western European individuals who deracinated themselves from the community by excessive cults of individualism, subjectivism and individual independence. Adam Smith's idea of reptilian competition in economy must have been inspired by the mentality of the atomised and aggressive individuals of the North Western Europe. This mentality of ruthless individual competitiveness particularly developed in areas which never experiences Ancient Rome's cults such as "humanitas" and "familia". Even to day Mediterranean capitalism is less ruthless than the Anglo-American one.

Adam Smith's idea of individual competition in economy must have inspired Herbert Spencer's idea of competition in sociology. Perhaps, it also inspired Malthus's idea of competition in demography and the Darwinian idea of competition in evolutionary biology. These beliefs are all still part of Western Culture, in spite of clear evidence that all living matter, from bacteria to the most advanced multicellular organisms, is based on the cooperation of a variety of factors on local and global levels, and in spite of evidence that we are a special social species which developed a brain capable of the most rational cooperation, caring, loving and nurturing.

Like any other political system, democracy lays down moral, legal and economic conditions which facilitate the formation of an elite or a ruling class, which class has a keen interest to perpetuate the system. In a democracy, the most selfish and unscrupulous, the most treacherous and fraudulent, have a better chance of success. Democracy's ruling class created a culture which transforms reptilian characteristics into virtues. This elite creates their own circle, their own establishment, their own enclosure and their own territory, all to suit their prominent reptilian legacy.

Western style democracy and its capitalist economy placed woman in an inferior position because, by nature and by her superior mental development, she is less competitive, less aggressive, less violent and less reptilian than man.

Therefore we are left with a paradox: we have woman who by nature is more democratic than man, the victim of democracy. This paradox can be explained if we take into consideration the important fact that Western style democracy is dominated by capitalist economy which is more hierarchical than democratic.

Western democracy invented the wishful idea of

individual equality. But, in reality, democracy and liberal capitalism are man's games, invented and played by man when woman was man's chattel and before woman acquired any political or economic rights. Like any other game, democracy and liberal capitalism were invented and practiced by those who were and are successful in these games. Playing their own games with their own rules, on their own ground, gives men an advantage over women.

There cannot be equality between man and woman in these games mainly due to their differences in mental developments. These games are based on ruthless competition, extreme individual self-interest and excessive individual selfishness, all more in the nature of man's reptilian mentality than in woman's more mature, more caring and more community orientated mentality. In fact, woman's mentality is an ideal breeding ground in which to help man in his unscrupulous exploitation and in his Darwinian attitude.

What is even more negative with competitive games, is that man develops an extra fear, the fear of losing. This increased fear creates extra nervous energy thus extra aggression, extra selfishness and extra self-centredness. This added fear of losing returns us to the primitive existence in which our superior brains cannot realise that, however exciting it might be, in competition we lose precious time, the time to live and enjoy life.

Forcing the wishful idea of equality between woman and man into reality, destroys sociality, togetherness and the sense of community. Equals do not bond. They even reject each other, as they are afraid of each other. In fact, equality creates animosity, negative to complementarity, participation, sharing or tolerance, so essential in reducing an individual's physical and mental instability or discomfort to minimal levels.

Equality is contrary to calming and protective intimacy, dialogue, co-operation and intercourse. By nature, equality is sterile and sterility is not fruitful. Without fruitfulness there is no future.

We invented the wishful belief that we are all equal in the eyes of God. Why then did God not create us equal in the first place? He did not create us equal because He came into existence after millions of years of evolution. He appeared with the human mind and its wishful beliefs.

Women do not need man's games. What they need is political and economic order thereby allowing them to get on with life and be more mature and more humane, more loving and more caring, all in the interest of the whole community, thereby helping men to become more serious, more mature and more humane. This would bring about a better future, a safer planet and a pleasanter life on it.

Better conditions for a more mature and a more humane humanity could be achieved by replacing democracy, which leans on power, with contributocracy which leans on authority. As I explained, the difference between power and authority is while the former stems from the clouds of the mind, its beliefs and ideologies, the latter has its roots firmly on the ground. Being rootless, power is ruthless and destructive, while authority is fruitful and benevolent.While power is feared, authority is respected. Power is feared because it has no control over itself. Power is shameless. It is shameless because it is immature.

Authority is respected because it implies a personal sacrifice, dedication or contribution towards others and the community. Being respected, authority becomes a model, an example to imitate.

Contributocracy is based on the valorisation of an individual's contribution to the community and its welfare. As everyone and anyone is able to contribute to the interest of the community, everyone and anyone can be the maker of his or her own excellence, his or her worth or merit, his or her authority.

Even the most community-dependent person can achieve merit, or contribute to the community, quite simply by gratitude. Gratitude develops modesty and moderation which reduces both abuse and the exploitation of the community's benefits. In fact, contributocracy offers a fair equality of opportunities to everyone.

We are a species whose culture and its values play an important part, mainly because we are the most fragile and undeveloped species regarding our innate patterns of behaviour. Due to our uncertain inborn drives is why we developed culture and cultural values. We also acquired the capability of imitation, another sign of our poorly developed innate patterns of behaviour.

Our cultural values influence us so much that we create powerful biochemical reactions in our body and brain. Evidence of this can be seen in our psychosomatic diseases as well as our psychosomatic well-being.

We can create our cultural values with the wishfulness of our mind which is under the influence of our desired self, of our inflated ego. Our cultural values can also be created by our mature brain.

Being wishful, the cultural values created by the mind place us in a state of anxiety and fear, as they place us above and against reality and nature.

The mature brain's contributocracy, in which we follow the natural and realistic law that without investing or planting to-day there will be no dividends or crops tomorrow, can only be in our interest and in the best interest of the future life on our planet.

Man has to replace his mind's wishful hope and prayers for a better future with the mature brain's reasoning that a better future is in our hands, in our present sacrifices and contributions for the sake of the community and the environment.

Man must replace his wishful belief in the paradise of after-life, a futile belief, anyway because man sold his soul in exchange for material wealth in this world. It is also a futile belief because if in its deviousness his soul has succeeded in reaching "paradise", it would find that "paradise" was a barren desert. The religious fanatics who reached there, in accordance with their religious beliefs, despise work because work denigrates their importance and even the most prosperous planet or "paradise" becomes barren if it is not worked, nurtured or taken care of.

Democracy divides the community into atomised and lonely individuals. In order to reduce the fear of loneliness, these isolated individuals form gangs or political factions which, creating hostilities, divides the community even more. Democracy, in fact, basically ends in partitocracy, gangs at war resulting in one gang becoming the

195

government.

In democracy people is ruled, in contributocracy everyone can rule himself, everyone can become respected authority by becoming authority over himself, by eliminating subjectivism, selfishness and self-centredness.

Being orientated around contributions to others and to the community, contributocracy would unite individuals in a safer and more protective community. Reducing fears and anxieties, contributocracy would allow humane brain to come into prominence.

But, what is very important is that while in a democracy it is the most ruthless human element which comes into power and prominence, in contributocracy, the most humane and mature people will become influential.

Using Darwinian language, one could say that in a community in which humaneness dominates, natural selection would favour the survival and reproduction of humane humans. This, in fact, should coincide with natural law which knows that the fittest only achieve maximum fitness in maturity. In our present culture the fittest seem to be the most immature and ruthless.

One of the most significant negative sides of democracy is that it creates discontent. It creates discontent because it makes broken promises, unfulfilled expectations and disillusions. Contrary to other animal's physical needs, which are satiable, the needs of man's mind or desires are insatiable. Our desires are insatiable because whenever a desire is fulfilled it increases our ego's importance which increases its pretensions. These escalate our desires. Gratification of the mind's desires expands desires. In view of this, Bertrand Russell's definition of individual freedom is empty of real sense. He insisted that individual freedom consists of "an absence of obstacles to the realisation of our desires." As our desires are insatiable, pursuing freedom only reduces us into deep melancholia. In order to solve the problem of the escalating ego's desires, man invented belief in miracles, praying to an omnipotent God, invented by his mind and its wishful desires.

By cultivating the individual's desires and expectations, democracy prevents us from cultivating our real potential on which we could reach contentment. Contributocracy creates togetherness which implies modesty and moderation and this is the source of healthy energy and contentment.

In fact, we only reach higher levels of healthy contentment when we involve ourselves below our full capabilities. Increasing our capabilities we increase our potential for more contentment and the joy of living. On the other hand, increasing our pretensions or involvements in activities which are above our capabilities, opens the way to a life of stress, discontent and distress.

In contributocracy, an individual's political and electoral rights would be related to the individual's level of merit. These merits should be calculated by the community on the basis of the worth of an individual's contribution to the community welfare. Particular appreciation should be rewarded for voluntary benevolent work in the social services. People in this work should have extra electoral votes.

Contributing to the procreation and perpetuation of life and carrying a deeper sense of responsibility towards life and life's habitat, women should also be entitled to an extra electoral vote each.

We often discuss the next generations and their future. There is, however, no legal representative of the next generations and their interests in our present political system. The only possible and obvious representatives of future generations are present day mothers. To protect the next generations, a mother should be entitled to an extra voting right, in all community's elections, for each child under the electoral age.

It is easy to criticise this idea by pointing out that many women would procreate as many children as possible in order to increase their benefits and their political influence. The answer to this is that contributocracy can only work validly in a culture dominated by maturity, in which shame limits excesses. Shame is a part of woman, as long as she is not trying to imitate the selfish and exploiting mentality of immature man. In fact, throughout history, whenever women have been in prominence and respected,

197

there are signs of a shame-culture, of limited individual selfishness and self-interest.

Teachers, judges, medical doctors, nurses and those who contribute to the community's physical,mental, social, political, economic and environmental sanity and stability, should also have an extra 2 to 5 electoral votes, the exact amount depending on the importance of their particular contributions to the community's welfare and its future.

In contributocracy the media will have a particularly prominent place as it can contribute a great deal to the community and its interest by exposing individual excessive self-interest or pretentiousness.

With just one electoral vote per person, democracy wanted to give absolute importance to the individual, who, in fact, became the pillar of the system. This equality opened the way to ruthless competition for inequality. By now, many people are realising that the system based on primitive reptilian characteristics is not working in the interest of humanity, of our planet, or the life on it.

The significant advantage of contributocracy, however, would be that man's demagogy and rethoric, which are highly successful in democracy and other wishful ideologies, would lose their seductive power.

There are certain people in our present culture trying to improve the life in our reptilian jungle, by imploring for some humanitarianism. The difference between the present culture's humanitarianism, however and the new culture's humaneness, is that while the former tries to help others on the expenses of others, the latter will aim to improve oneself, at the expense of oneself. Humanitarianism is an ideology merely achieving its own negation when it strives to impose itself on reality, to become coercive. Humaneness, however, is a need of our mature brain, a natural and spontaneous drive in search of gratification and contentment. Humanitarianism is not necessarily humane.

Many people claim that the troubles humanity face are caused by the gap between our present culture's ideologies and beliefs and reality, insisting that we should find an equilibrium between the two. This is impossible due to the expansive nature of the mind's beliefs and ideologies.

There is only one way to solve our problem and this is to abandon our immature culture for a mature one. A mature culture is in perfect tune with nature.

To those who might consider my theory nonsense, I answer that the alternative is an even more chaotic life. More and more women are imitating men's ruthless, selfish and self-centred mentality which is bringing more and more fear to men, which will induce even more cynicism. By now, our culture is already producing more and more cynical children.

Obsessed by equality with men, some women are already reaching a tragi-comic aspiration: joint armed forces. This implies that women will be sent to war to kill other soldiers in the name of men's abstract beliefs or ideologies. To kill life is contrary to woman's nature which consists of giving life, nurturing it and caring for it. Perhaps, this is why, when women achieve success in their competition with men, they are seldom happy.

Recently women are achieving another pathetic equality with men: they are starting to practice man's rough games, such as boxing and wrestling. To see women fighting, using brute force against each other, is not in their nature. That is why they are so pathetic.

Mature women are not supposed to be figures of fun. We might laugh if we saw a man slip on a banana skin, but not a pregnant woman. A man falling about drunk is cause for amusement, but a woman in the same condition is pathetic or embarrassing.

The madness brought about by our present culture is evident in the fact that more and more people live their lives by mainly concentrating on temporary excitements and instant orgasms, which are followed by long spans of a drained, dazed or groggy existence or by post-orgasmic emptiness or depression. More and more women, in fact, are becoming obsessed with reaching equality with men and to be able to have an orgasm. A multiple orgasm is able to give a woman a sense of superiority, which, in essence, is the aim of equality.

Competition aims at victory and victory leaves

victims. Any gain is someone's loss in our present culture. A primitive mind builds its sense of superiority on the victims of gain.

Many people explain that it is the pessimistic vision of the future which justifies the present life of excitements and fun. Could it not be more accurate to stress that it is the life of excitements and fun that sees the future in such uncertain terms? In post-excitement emptiness the future cannot but be empty.

The life of excitements has brought another negative side-effect: a passion for changes. This passion or obsession for novelties tends to expand and accelerate which also expands and accelerates disorientation and destabilisation. In fact, we are excited by novelties because they carry uncertainties, which bring anxieties and fears. These anxieties and fears revive our reptilian legacy. Perhaps, this is why our passions tend to be so wild.

I would like to remind those who might doubt that women in prominence could improve life and its conditions on this planet, that the tragedies of life on our planet in the past and at present were caused by man's pretension to create a better world using his fantasies and by becoming a fanatical believer of his fantasies, often calling them "prophecies" or "revelations".

Woman is less fanatical. Fanaticism is very much in tune with our reptilian legacy of obtuse and blind stubbornness. Woman's limbic system and her new brain are less influenced by our species' reptilian inheritance than man's.

Women come into prominence in periods of crises because the crises are generally created by men. When men fail in their infantile or adolescent fantasies, they run to their mothers, wives, mistresses, or daughters for comfort and advice.

Soon man might have no choice but to accept woman's common sense in politics. Man's game of democracy and his other political ideologies is coming to an end. In its expansion towards its final explosion, liberal capitalism is destroying its political protector, liberal democracy.

200

CAPITALISM VERSUS DEMOCRACY

Western style democracy is slowly becoming a humble servant of liberal capitalism. Western democracy, along with many other forms of government, is being more and more manipulated by economy. Economy has succeeded in convincing humanity that its growth is the supreme value and must dominate any other. Next to economy's expansion, politics, morals, aesthetics or ecology play very minor parts. We are all aware that economic growth and our obsession for material possessions can damage our quality of life, pollute the planet and increase crime and violence, but no-one dares to try and conquer this obsession.

By reducing the political power of democracy, liberal capitalism has reduced political control over the individual's rights and above all over individual economic freedom, thereby increasing the ruthless rat-race. But, this of course is the supreme interest of liberal capitalism and its growth. In this growth, liberal capitalism eliminates politics, society and the State. It eliminates the community's rights and public interest.

In a world which is based on material values and wealth, it is obvious that the individual's political rights will be more powerful in those who are better off than in those who are less well off. Given the fact that the former is a minority and that the latter a majority, Western democracy is a far cry from being democratic. In the U.S.A., where people's personal values are related to his or her wealth, the rich have a greater chance of being elected to the offices of public interest.

What makes Western democracy even less democratic is the fact that the representatives of capitalism who rule over the majority are not even elected. What's more, they are selected in the most ruthless Darwinian way.

The conflict between political public interest and economic private interest is evident in the policy of employment. We have a growing number of unemployed people which is in the interest of capitalist economy, because this implies a lower cost of labour, thus a lower cost of production, implying better competitiveness, bringing higher profits which serve to perpetuate and expand capitalism and its dominance over any other power.

In a capitalist democracy even justice is not just, as it tends to only gratify those who can afford it.

Western democracy invented a powerful weapon in its idea of equality; to give everyone over 18 the right to vote in elections. Being ruled by capitalist economy, democracy's political equality is a puerile decoration for those in search of self-importance, a decoration which merely amuses the real rulers.

What is more, democracy's illusion of equality can be damaging, particularly to young people in search of their first job. Being unable to find work, they develop a feeling of personal inadequacy, a feeling of failure.

In order to remain in power, democracy has to expand. This is done by pleasing the electorate's desires, by inflating the individuals' political rights.

As the economy cannot fulfil the expectations promised by the inflated political rights, most of the politicians in power are blamed for it and often replaced with other politicians who in turn promise even more inflated political rights.

In order to make the vicious circle even more vicious, politicians try to solve the problem by increasing the budget deficit or public borrowing. Losing elections, the politicians who created national debts find a certain satisfaction in seeing their opponents's economic policy collapsing because of the amount of national debts.

Some politicians even inserted the individual's right to work in their Constitutions. This is derided by the millions of unemployed in most Western democracies.

Apologists of democracy claim that it is influenced by public opinion. This may be true, but public opinion is also easily influenced by the mass-media which is either in the hands of the capitalists or manipulated by capitalist economy. Depending either directly or indirectly on private capital, it is only logical that the mass-media will select, interpret and present information in a way as to please those who provide its existence.

One of the greatest achievements of capitalism was to convince public opinion that an individual's self-interest is in the public interest and that the best democracy, one in which the government, this guardian of public interest, is the least powerful and that any government's intervention or interference in an individual's ruthless self-interest is not in the interest of the public.The government is entitled to intervene in economy, however, when, invited to by selfish private interest.

We live with the comic fallacy that ruthless private interest is in public interest, that stock-markets' or currency free markets' speculations are healthy and that the gamblings of commodity brokers are in the interest of deprived Third World countries.

An individual of Western democracy no longer feels he belongs to a State and even less that he is protected by its government. He feels alone with his self-interest. A citizen's loyalty towards the State and his solidarity with other members of society, are not in tune with the opportunism, inspired by self-interest. The State and other citizens of the State are there to be exploited by the capitalist "homo oeconomicus", to its furthest extreme. Exploitation is his supreme aim, an aim which justifies any means. Exploitation is the supreme aim because its goal is material success, which, in our present materialistic mentality, justifies anything.

Democracy, which, because of its flexibility, was supposed to be an ideal political system in our changing world, has been overpowered by the rigid tyranny of economic capitalism.

The dominance of liberal capitalism is evident in Western democracy's field of education. Instead of educating children to become decent, civilised, humane and mature people, we educate them to become primitive, ruthless, selfish and aggressive monsters. In schools and at home, particularly in the U.S.A., where liberal capitalism is most prominent, children are indoctrinated to be self-confident, self-assertive, competitive and aggressive and to believe in sacrosanct unrestrained self-interest. These

203

characteristics, which are in tune with our primitive brain, are the essential pillars of liberal capitalism. The ideal "homo oeconomicus" of liberal capitalism is a reptilian minded man.

Fewer and fewer well-mannered, caring and gentle young people can find jobs these days, because they are not aggressive enough, therefore appear economic loses.

In our present culture, dominated by liberal capitalism and its cruel materialism, it is very sad that children are taught more about how to achieve proficiency or economic efficiency, how to be able to score off and take advantage of others, than about sociality, togetherness, cooperation, friendship, sympathy, empathy, caring, loving and sharing.

The new generations of human beings are taught how to exploit their fellow human beings rather than how to understand them and how to abuse nature rather than how to respect and enjoy it.

We use knowledge to transform robots into human beings. By not using it properly, we have instead transformed humans into robots, or what is even more humiliating, we have transformed humans into the obedient servants of robots. Could it perhaps be that we are attracted by robots because they are very much in tune with our reptilian legacy.

We are assisting in a tragi-comic situation as far as our ecological crisis is concerned. Everyone is aware that we are slowly heading towards a catastrophe. No politician or government, however, can do anything to stop or to alleviate the crisis, as no-one dares to go against the sacredness of economic growth. No politician or government would dare to point out that economic expansion has reached a point in which it is counter-productive, that its growth merely serves itself. This is dangerous because in our Machiavellian mentality we consider that the aim justifies the means. Sadly the Machiavellian mentality does not take into consideration that our planet's means are by now, seriously limited.

We have transformed our land, rivers and lakes, our seas and the atmosphere, in fact our entire habitat into a garbage tip. Living amongst garbage we have acquired the garbage mentality, in which beauty is irritating, thus vandalised, humaneness means simple-mindedness, wisdom implies naivety and cleanliness stinks. For this mentality, vulgarity means strength, body-building is beautiful, violence exciting, thus attractive and smartens means intelligence.

Many people think they are solving the problem of their environmental or ecological conscience by decorating and adopting external signs in order to impress. They march in the streets with banners entitled "Save the Planet", or T shirts endorsed with inscriptions such as: "Protect Wild Life". All in tune with their reptilian inheritance.

The subordination of politics in the interests of economy can be best seen in public services, particularly with public transport. Western governments have all failed in their public transport policies because they felt obliged to bow to economic expansion through the king of their industries, the automobile. If half of the capital invested by governments into the improvement of roads and motorways, was put into public transport instead, the quality of our lives and our mental and physical sanity would be in far better shape.

The monthly sales figures of new automobiles are monitored with trepidation, as they influence the stock-market, the rise or fall of the value of national currency on money markets and government policy. The ridiculous side of our economic and political life can be seen if we take into consideration that the demand for new motor-cars is often determined by people's status symbols, by excitements provided by new gadgets on the car and by the potential speed of the unnecessarily powerful engine, particularly as the speed-limit on roads is far lower than the speed that the car will go. Ridicule is further increased when it is taken into consideration that at least half the cars owned are not really needed and that half of the remaining half are often only used unnecessarily, polluting the atmosphere and creating accidents, besides limiting the efficiency of public transports.

The ugly side of the expansion of the economy through growth in the automobile industry is that politicians are forced to adapt urbanism and its policy to the needs of this industry. Motor-car circulation and parking spaces have priority over anything else including public parks and even children's playgrounds.

As I said before, in order to placate the economy and its expansion, politicians are able to commit the most atrocious crime: the stimulation of demand through the policy of cheap credit which encourages people into debt, thus destabilising their future.

The public health services in many capitalist countries are influenced by powerful pharmaceutical industries rather than by the politicians in charge of National Health.

With their long debates and lengthy discussions amongst their committees, the national parliaments of democratic countries are too clumsy to cope with the rapidity of international markets operations and their travelling speed, this new wealth of the economy. The total irrelevance of parliaments' discussions can best be seen during currency crises when instant decisions have to be taken.

We are a laughable species because we are pretentious. Pretentiousness blinds us, making us behave in an insensitive and ridiculous way. By nature, we are a social species but we spend our whole lives fighting the community and its spirit, in the name of the cult of individualism and individual autonomy. When we achieve this individual autonomy we sink to the precariousness of loneliness and isolation. It is on this lonely and isolated existence that we build our capitalist economy. This economy is ruled by the material values determined by the market, a market without past or future and without civility or humaneness. This omnipotent and omnipresent new god, this ruthless and primitive capitalist market dictates the value of everything in material terms. Pricing everything in material terms, the market corrupts, trivialises and vulgarises aesthetic and ethical values and ecological and humane considerations.

The pathetic side of the capitalist economy's market is evident when we consider that its activity mainly consists of the behaviour or attitudes of frightened lonely individuals, easily manipulated by the ruthless human element which play the market in search of excitement and instant profit.

Some economists insist that liberal market economy is based on utilitarianism, the economic behaviour of any individual, being ruled by the maximalisation of personal utility. But the level of the utility is determined by the mind and its ego's desires, which vary from individual to individual. That is why our behaviour is unpredictable. Lacking predictability, our economy is not a science: it has more exceptions than laws. The economy of other species would be a science, however, because it is predictable.

Most of the time utilitarianism is nothing but a here and now ruthless expediency which lacks self-respect and dignity and this prevents us from considering other human beings with respect and civility. In instant utilitarianism other human beings are commodities.

The utilitarianism of a mature humanity would consist of personal investments and sacrifices in view of a better future and long term dividends.

There is no such thing as an objective utility. It is our mind with its desires and its ego's caprices which attribute utility to objects.

We attribute values to things in relation to our desires. These desires expand with gratification because the gratification of our desires inflate our sense of importance. It is the expansion of desires that makes our mind attribute utility and values to even the most useless things or objects. The mind justifies this irrationality by developing an absurd belief that the unnecessary is beautiful and that useless objects can be decorative, thus impressing others. A vast proportion of people to-day pay millions of pounds and even more dollars for a totally unnecessary and even ugly painting, for example, in order to lock it away in a safe for the rest of their lives, to leave it to their children or grand-children, who will probably often sell it to buy drugs or a Ferrari. The power of vanity, a mental disorder which most of us suffer from, can be seen in the prices we pay for fashionable impressionist paintings at auctions.

"Individuals know their own interest best," goes the motto of liberal capitalism. Most individuals live in a world of the mind's wishful illusions and pretensions which is not in the best interest of anyone on this planet and above all of

207

its future.

Prisons are overcrowded with individuals who knew best. To-day, the increasing number of mentally disturbed, chronically depressed and suicidals, is made up of those who thought they knew best.

To-day's tragedy of humanity is that we do not seek a cure for the mental disorder created by our illusions and pretensions as this might interfere with our present life of excitements, which we consider in our best interest. But, times are changing. Those who justified their immaturity by repeating the famous motto "Après moi le déluge," cannot continue, as "le déluge" is not coming after us, "le déluge" is already with us. We are already sinking into a "déluge" of garbage and pollution.

By becoming international, the liberal market has become an even more omnipresent and omnipotent divinity in front of which politicians world-wide are impotent and slow to cope with its ever more instant operations.

No politician of any country who cares for his career and they all do, would dare, for the sake of the public interest of his country or in the name of better global ecology, to oppose or to protest against the interest of the international markets or the interest of multinational corporations and their economies. There is no country in the world which could save its currency with its monetary reserves against an attack in the world markets by international speculators. Such is the impotence of politicians.

The sovereignty of the nation-State has been reduced in an economy dominated by the international market and multinational corporations. The globalisation of the economy has degraded the sovereignty of the present form of the nation-State in one of its vital essentials, its power to manipulate taxation independently. With the free movements of humans and capitals and with international fiscal competition, which globalisation of economy implies, a great deal of the nation-State's freedom of manipulation of its fiscal and monetary policies is limited.

Thrown into global economy, many people develop even deeper fears because this reduces their sense of identity and their sense of belonging. Reducing the relevance of the nation-State and its government, the globalisation of the economy has contributed and continues to contribute, to the political disintegration of big States into smaller political units based on a more intimate local identity and belonging. Closer systems are less unstable and less uncertain.

The globalisation of economy also increases an individual's fears for another reason. It eliminates national boundaries, it eliminates the sense of territory, a feeling of home.

The European Community, which best proves my explanation, is now trying to increase this trend of the disintegration of nation-States into smaller regional or local communities by creating a common European currency, the Ecu. Forcing the Ecu on people could create animosity or even hatred of it. This could prevent saving and increase spending and inflation. The Ecu could become like chips in casinos, ready to be thrown away on the gambling tables, as this plastic money does not provide a feeling of mutual belonging. In fact, many people might think twice before gambling if they had to gamble with real money.

The internationalisation of economy brings yet another fear, the fear of increasing international unemployment. This fear is particularly stressful because there is nobody to blame for it. International economy takes no responsibility for anyone but its own self-interest.

The internalisation of economy and of multinational corporations contributes to another stressful factor for which nobody seems responsible, the deterioration of ecological conditions on our planet.

The nation-State's validity and its protective capacity of its citizens has been eroded by the internationalisation of national wealth. National wealth is more and more of a financial nature which makes it easily transferable in the global economy. Becoming free and stateless, this national wealth easily emigrates towards more favourable climates.

The internationalisation of national wealth also restricts the protective feeling of national territory.

Citizens of nation-States who are members of international political or economic communities of States, increase their unease and fears because their national parliaments' legislative power is more and more absorbed by the executive power of the international community's administration which power is greatly influenced by invisible international bureaucracy, which, like any other bureaucracy, carries its genetic disease which consists of corruptibility.

The most active and influential human element of capitalist economies belong more to the international business community and its laws and ethics than to those of their individual   nation.For the individuals of the international business community, any national sovereignty is nothing but a commodity, often bought as his convenient fiscal domicile.

Western capitalism and its international free market carry a great responsibility for the economic and political instabilities of many undeveloped countries. The present and the future of many of these countries are decided by ruthless speculators, gambling in the world commodity market.

The World Bank and the International Monetary Fund would have done better for the economic and political stabilities of these countries if, instead of giving them financial aid or credit, they had established stabler, more dignified and fairer prices for the commodities produced by these underdeveloped countries. One can visualise the dealers of commodity markets, in say, London or Chicago, just for the excitement of gambling, reducing millions to misery in seconds.

The United Nations which are responsible for the international political stability could reach their aim far better if they imposed a stability and fairness onto the prices of the commodities produced by poorer countries.

The United Nations could help the world economy and political stability in another significant way. They should prohibit the export of arms of any kind from one country to another. This would enable the governments of developed countries to resist the pressure of the powerful arms industry.

Exporting arms is positively damaging the world economy and the ecology as a whole. Arms create tension and wars which are destructive. Damages to the world economy and to the ecology by wars are far higher than the amount of benefices realised by the exporting countries.

The post-capitalist economy should be run by the local community for the sake of the community as a whole. A community can only have a sense of the community if it is limited to a small municipal level where people have a better chance to know each other and belong to each other.

Most main industries and services within the grounds of a municipality should be municipalised. In a small community sharing the economy and work is more easily accomplished.

The role of the nation-State or of a federation of States should be the protection of the autonomies of the local authorities. This is in fact, the only way for central governments to acquire authority and independence from the economy's dominance. By the devolution of its power, a central government acquires authority, so needed by a referee for potential conflicts among local communities.

The bigger the State or association of States, the higher is people's need to belong and to be protected by a smaller community. Even national languages tend to be replaced by the more intimate local dialects.

The bigger the State, the more complex it is. The more complex the State, the more unstable it is. The more unstable it is, the more restless it is. The more restless it is, the more expansive it is. Any increase in expansion increases complexity, restlessness, agitation and aggression. The smaller the community, the lesser is its instability. Even in the present chaotic and neurotic capitalist rat-race, some smaller communities show more stability and serenity. The best examples of these are Luxembourg, Liechtenstein, Andorra, Monaco and San Marino. In smaller communities there is less individual fearful anonimity and less individual madness with its typical excessive selfishness and self-centredness.

The future cannot be safe in the hands of either nationalised economy or in those of private economy. The former is run by the ever increasing inefficient, incompetent and corrupt bureaucracy and its own instant interest, the latter by independent individuals also for their own here and now personal self-interest. International corporations are even less in the interest of the public, because they are so far removed from any community or State. They are run by individuals who only belong to the corporation in which they work, making them unable to have any other loyalty or consideration but that of their corporation and their own pockets.

An international corporation does not serve anyone's interest but that of its own expansion. Being an obsession, this expansion is short sighted. This short-sightedness makes for a black future, as it creates international pollution, international unemployment and a universal ecological crisis.

International corporation is a perfect example of liberal capitalist economy as it serves only its capital's pursuit of the maximalisation of profit by maximal exploitation of everything and everyone, including its own rulers, its own employees and the planet's limited natural resources.

Multinational corporation is the supreme achievement of capital and capitalism, which consists of freedom from accountability to anybody but to their own growths. We should not forget that multinational corporations have contributed to internationally validate capitalism's wishful belief that any intervention of the public interest in the private unrestrained maximalisation of the profit is not in public interest.

Multinational corporations seem to have inspired multinational blocks or certain types of super-States. With the dominance of the economy over politics and with our present capitalist exploiting mentality, these communities of States cannot last long due to the tendency of each member-State to expand its exploitation and profit on the expenses of the super-State and of other members of the super-State.

The post-capitalist economy will enter into a new set of values, values related to contribution to the community's welfare. This set of values will replace economy from its present ruling position to that of the servant of the community.

The community's valorisation will rule values. The values of a social species should be determined by the community's interest as a whole, in which the economy plays a part but not the dominant one. When the economy becomes the predominant value, no other value can stop its obsessive expansion on the expenses of all other values.

Toppling down the economy from its tyrannical pedestal will enable many women to exercise their maturity better. The present capitalist economy is a man's game which is in tune with his reptilian mentality. Liberal capitalist economy helps the perpetuation of man's immature mentality on the expenses of women, children and the future of our planet.

By enabling woman to become less dependent on man and of his game, she will be in a position to use her better developed brain. Lately, certain scientists are convinced that woman's wider, more pragmatic and more equilibrated way of reasoning is due to the more solidly built corpus callosum, the band of cells uniting the cerebral hemispheres. We seldom appreciate woman's way of reasoning because, in his dominance, man has succeeded to falsify his defects as human virtues, glorifying defects such as philosophising, fantasizing and idealising.

Man also glorifies his sense of duty and honour which in essence, means serving his wishful ideologies, beliefs or other fantasies, in the most servile way, placing him in the sad uniqueness of the animal world, that of killing and exterminating, persecuting and torturing members of his own species.

Instead of imitating man, woman will be herself. This might help man to advance towards maturity and seriousness by imitating woman. As I stressed before, in maturity man becomes maternal, therefore caring.

I realised how sad life created and perpetuated by man's prepotency was, when I was researching mothers' emotions caused by the discovery that their new-born child is a boy and by the news that the new-born baby is a girl. Many women described that their first sensation on discovering that they had produced a boy was one of looking at a stranger, even a hostile intruder. But, with a baby girl, these women felt an immediate intimacy, togetherness, a physical part of themselves, a continuation or a perpetuation of themselves.

213

EPILOGUE

In its blinding arrogance, man's speculative world of wishful beliefs and ideologies could not but create a life of tragi-comedy which finds its best expression in irony. In fact, many people consider themselves victims of the "irony of fate". They fail to realise, however, that this irony of fate takes place in a world of faith. Irony is part of the world of faith because most of the time faith is fake, it is bad faith. Faith is in bad faith because it is preceded and inspired by pretentiousness, a pretentious desire above our merits. The irony of fate is, in fact, a result of natural justice, a punishment for pretentiousness over reality.

In order to reach our individual autonomy, through material possessions and wealth, we have adopted the capitalist economy. But our cult of individual autonomy implies an escape from the humane achievements of our social species which are: caring, compassion, togetherness, sharing and serenity. Escaping into the cult of individual autonomy we have gone back to our reptilian existence, to a Hobbesian war of all against all.

We have adopted the ruthlessness of capitalist economy in order to achieve riches. One of our present culture's major principles is "to have is to be." To a primitive mind, possessions are exciting and excitement is the supreme aspiration of those who escape from the serenity of the mature world.

But, the big irony of fate! More and more people now realise that we have sold our souls for material wealth and have reached a stage in which we have no soul, only huge individual and national debts.

In global terms, capitalism has succeeded in creating more poverty than wealth, more discontent than happiness, more injustice than justice. Above all, capitalism has impoverished and continues to impoverish our planet, our children and their children's living habitat.

In our obsession for economic growth we fail to realise that the supposition that economic growth creates jobs is merely the wishfulness of the obsessed. Figures provided by the United Nations Development Programme show that since 1960 economic growth has created "jobless growth". Since 1960, in the United Kingdom, the economy grew by 83 percent, but employment has fallen by 6 percent. The relative figures in Germany were: 122 per cent and 15 per cent. A similar trend can be seen in the U.S.A. and in developing countries such as India and Pakistan.

In spite of all this, many people still call man "sapiens". Some even call him "sapiens, sapiens," whatever this may mean! Perhaps his ability to impress himself with his own wishful beliefs and in spite of his increasing consumption of sleeping pills, tranquillisers, alcohol and narcotic drugs.

Having shaken our ethical values, the economy has opened the way to another serious danger: the unrestrained expansion of science. This expansion of science is seriously dangerous because, instead of helping us to understand nature and harmonise with its order, science and scientists find their thrills in trying to change or dominate nature, its laws and its order, which, in essence, implies trying to destroy nature and build a new one in pretentious man's image. After all, the first male divinity, the Mesopotamian supreme God, Marduk, had to kill the supreme goddess, his mother, in order to replace her with himself.

In violating nature, science has created an atmosphere of tension, animosity and enmity. In this atmosphere, more and more people are developing antagonism towards science and are starting to distrust and fear scientists.

What is more, science has reached a point beyond which the benefices of its achievements are in most cases far inferior to the cost of their side effects. For instance, it continues trying to prolong our life-span "ad infinitum", without taking into consideration that people over the age of 85, steadily increasing in number in most cases are dependent on an already indebted State.

We are finally beginning to realise that what we considered the brilliant scientific discoveries of artificial fertilisers and pesticides have in fact brought about far more damage than benefit.

I would not be surprised if one day the unrestrained expansion of science results in the persecution of scientists.

Science seldom informs us of the major scientific evidence that nature reacts violently to its abuses and punishes its pretentious aims at subduing or violating it. Science knows, but seldom informs us, that nature fights back. Science also knows, but seldom explains, that nature is only obliging when nurtured and cared for.

More and more people are starting to realise that much of to-day's unemployment is due to scientific and technological discoveries aiming at higher economic productivity using machinery. Soon this will reach the tragi-comic situation of an over-abundance of goods, with few able to afford them.

Many countries have erected science museums, proudly exhibiting the achievements of science. It might be interesting to erect museums showing the failures of science. One of its major failures is that it has increased our anxieties and fears, anxieties and fears which prevent us from emancipating ourselves from our reptilian legacy.

When an individual of our social species escapes from his community in the name of his cult of individual freedom and independence, he loses the restraint or control of the community, the source of his common sense sanity, reasoning and mature values, which is yet another irony!

When a man escapes into his individual freedom, he becomes intoxicated by it. Like any other drug-addict, he becomes a slave to his freedom to the point of irrational servility.

Being a wishful idea, individual freedom craves to become reality, to prove itself by forcing itself onto reality, by destroying the natural order ruled by the laws of nature, which disallow any freedom but that of complying with them. In fact, our ecological crisis is mainly the work of man's pursuit of his individual freedom against the natural order.

Living with and among others, man's individual freedom can only be realised on the expenses of other people's freedom and this creates tension and aggression. it can also result in bloody and destructive revolutions which, most of the time, are fought in the name of someone's wishful idea of freedom against others' wishful ideas of freedom.

Like any other wishful belief, individual freedom tends to expand itself. In its expansion, individual freedom can reach another irony: fanaticism. In fact, much of our Western culture was created by fanatics.

What can be even more ironic is the fact that in its expansion individual freedom eventually explodes into anarchy. Reaching anarchy the fanatics of individual freedom invoke tyranny. Most revolutions which are created and conducted in the name of individual freedom end this way. After all, Hitler and Mussolini were democratically elected and acclaimed dictators.

This is the natural end of an unnatural wishful aspiration. Not being in the nature of the member of a social species, individual freedom is suicidal. Individual freedom carries the anxiety of precariousness as it lives on the edge of a precipice. Living with the anxiety created by precariousness, we cannot but behave irrationally. This is evident if we take into consideration that the more obsessed or fanatical an individual is about his freedom and autonomy, the more selfish and self-centred he becomes which is irrational for a member of a social species. Selfishness and self-centredness, for a member of a social species is, in fact, a mental disorder. What we usually call mental disorders are nothing but excessive selfishness and self-centredness caused by excessive individual freedom.

Unrestrained freedom reduces many people to suicide, another evidence of mental disorder, unique to our species in the phase of the mind's dominance, in the phase of the mind's capricious escape from maturity and serenity. In fact, many suicides are an escape into a precipice from the precarious existence on the edge of it. Like any other intoxication, the excitement of precariousness tends to grow into unbearable nightmares. In most suicides lies another irony of man's mind's world: an extreme materialisation of an individual's freedom, the freedom to end his own life. What a victory for "Homo sapiens." Like any victory, the victor is the victim of his own victory.

By committing suicide, perhaps man tries to punish the nature which he was unable to dominate. When he realises that life is not a gift of God but a burden imposed on him by nature, in his selfish immature way, he tries to off-load his burden by offending his offender. Such can be the pretentiousness of "Homo sapiens."

This madness should not be surprising as individual freedom is irrational in its very nature. Life is a necessity, a causal order determined by global interdependence, which does not allow freedom. In this world of causality, freedom is contrary to the very principle of life. The freedom of a cell would imply stopping its metabolism, the freedom of a heart would imply stopping its beating.

Our so glorified individual freedom is mainly a juvenile excitement created by the challenge of a causal order or a necessity. An occasional provocation or challenge of the natural order can bring some excitement and fun, but persevering in provocation and challenge implies a mental disorder. Provoking natural rationality is irrational.

Our main mental disorder started with our pretentiousness and our obsession with grandiosity. Pretentiousness develops fears that our wishful desires or hopes might not be gratified. These fears bring our reptilian legacy into prominence. This reptilian mentality uses our limbic brain and the neo-cortex in tune with its own logic and reasoning. Our two main brains which evolved in order to reduce the anxieties and fears of the reptilian brain, become instruments of this brain. Another irony!

When the reptilian mentality is in dominance, our memory, mainly the creation of the limbic brain, serves our reptilian needs and aspirations. When we are dominated by this reptilian mentality we only revoke facts and memories in accordance with the reptilian mentality of the given instant from our memory pool. An individual dominated by the selfish and self-centred reptilian mentality develops a limited egocentric memory on the expenses of a wider or more universal memory. A reptilian mentality creates its new memory by perceiving facts or experiences from external and internal worlds that suit this mentality.

What is particularly pathetic is that the sentimental and emotional capabilities of the limbic brain become instruments of the reptilian brain when in search of seduction, territory, wealth, power or conquest. Could it not be that the popular expression "crocodile tears" reflects the reptilian mentality's manipulation of emotions for instant exploitation or as an opportunistic expediency ?

In some parts of Western culture it is considered a real virtue to have a calculating control of ones personal emotions and to be able to exhibit opportunistic emotions to fit our reptilian expediency. Human hypocrisy is directly related to reptilian deviousness.

When our reptilian mentality dominates our other two brains, our neo-cortex capabilities of high reasoning, inventiveness and speech follow the logic and needs of the reptilian brain. Nazi philosophy, reasoning and oratory were all ruled by reptilian logic. The reptilian brain's logic, elaborated by the sophisticated neo-cortex, can in fact be devastating and catastrophic.

In tune with the deviousness of the reptilian mentality, the new brain's speech serves disinformation more than information. Being in tune with the reptilian tendency to decorate the appearance, disinformation is usually more successful than information.

From time to time religious leaders launch a new crusade against excessive selfishness and ruthless self-interest. These crusades give the impression of sad comedy because the actors are so blinded by their pretentiousness and performance that they do not see that they are acting to an empty theatre.

Absorbed into their free-for-all economic rat-race, which limits the efficiency of the senses, people do not even hear pompous sermons. Even if they did, they would not listen as they know that they are delivered by people who do not practice what they preach.

Many of these preachers advise us to return to past values, forgetting that it is these past values that created the roots of our present ones, the ones that carry the roots of the future.Those preaching the validity of religious values of the past conveniently forget religious wars, intolerance, persecutions, inquisitions and the tortures of the past. What is more, religious illusions inspire political fantasies.

219

Without Christ we would not have had Marx.

The mind's desires provide a major example of the tragic comedy which is the life of most of humanity.

Living in the precarious world of insatiable wishful desires, man develops a sense of impotence. Desires create a sense of impotence because they are usually far beyond our capabilities. In fact, prayers are the best evidence of impotence created by our wishful desires.

It is this man's sense of impotence that creates his desire for power.

Like any other insatiable wishful desire, the desire for power tends to expand and in its expanse, it increases man's impotence. That is why power can never achieve power over itself, its own self-control. That is why power usually ends in excess which brings it to its fall. Man's power is self-destructive. Power tries to hide its impotence behind a display of its importance. Vast monuments, churches or temples are erected as signs of man's prestige and importance. The colossal is powerful in the eyes of the impotent. Man builds big things in order to impress others, in order to seduce them or subdue them, in order to reduce or to placate his anxiety caused by his sense of impotence. In fact, many of the achievements of our civilisation have been inspired and created by man's sense of impotence. This is why a great deal of these achievements are unnecessary or sterile, a waste of human and natural resources. Financing illusions or dreams limits our planet's limited potential.

Excited by our pursuit of importance and prestige, we carry on spending enormous amounts of human and natural resources sending expensive rockets into space in order to have colour photographs of the moon and the planets. These exorbitantly priced picture post-cards should carry a message, however, saying: "Take care of your planet Earth, there is nothing as beautiful in the cosmos".

While our immature mentality pursues importance, prestige and power, our mature mentality pursues competence and excellence, the pillars of authority. Perhaps, this is why, while power intimidates, authority inspires affection and safety. While power is self-destructive, authority is self-constructive. Competence and excellence lean on moderation and it is this moderation which preserves our mental and physical sanity, which gives authority its self-constructiveness and stability. In fact, it is our lack of moderation, our eagerness and greed, all caused by pretentiousness, which are the most negative characteristics of our present mentality.

Our Western life and particularly life in the U.S.A. where wishful desires are even less restrained, is a neurotic life, a life of violence, cruelty and brutality. This is mainly due to the significant fact that we never exercise our capabilities with moderation. We exploit our capabilities to their extreme limits, which leaves us without any reserve capability. We exploit our capabilities to the maximum because our wishful desires and our pretentiousness are way beyond our capabilities of achieving them.

In fact, we are the victims of our capitalist mentality which consists of pursuing the exploitation of everything and everyone to extremes. We go so far in our exploiting mentality as to exploit our own capability to its extreme limits. Our capitalist economy and its working hours are created by man in order to exploit everything and everyone, merely to have a neurotic existence.

When our eagerness and greed exhaust the last reserves of our capabilities, of our healthy energy, we start living on nervous energy created by the extra fear that we develop having exhausted both our capabilities and our healthy energy.

Living on nervous energy, often helped by unhealthy stimulants or drugs, creates a life of violence and aggressiveness, brutality and toughness, impatience and intolerance, clumsiness and accidents, adventurousness and risk-taking, quarrels and litigations. In some countries where the life is even more neurotic, these litigations reach epidemic proportions.

Living on nervous energy creates anxieties, stress and stress related problems, as well as the disorder we call " a nervous breakdown".

Exhausting our reserve capabilities is particularly stressful in emergencies. Nature created these reserve capabilities for unpredictable dangers and lacking this reserve, panic can set in fast in any emergency.

Exhausting our capability reserve we reduce our reasoning and rationality to the level of our reptilian brain's instant opportunism.

Other animals seldom exploit their reserve capabilities to extreme limits. A predator, for example, will never consume its reserve capabilities in the pursuit of its prey, however hungry it might be. An animal will naturally try to conserve its reserve capabilities in case of a sudden emergency, of an unexpected attack by man or its own predator, This is what makes other animals more harmonious and graceful, more patient and tolerant than we are.

People with more reserve capability have a keener curiosity and a wider sense of observation which enriches the brain's activities.

Women, who are more mature and less pretentious than men, tend to preserve their reserve capability which renders them better equiped to cope with emergencies and crises than men. In fact, as I stressed before, one of the greatest historians, Ferdinand Gregorovius wrote: "It is indeed a remarkable historic phenomenon, that in periods of decadence some female figure generally rises into prominence."

Man, however, insists that his aggressiveness, competitiveness, violence and brutality, caused mainly by the capricious wishful desires of an inflated ego, are innate male drives, eternal and immutable because they are genetically determined.

These so-called "biological imperatives" disappear from the genes, however, when man reaches maturity!

Woman's reserve capability is also an important source of her better care for the future. This reserve capability enables her to invest parts of her present towards a better future. Ruthlessly exploiting his present to satisfy his instant desires, man tends to exhaust his reserve resources.

Our present Western farcical parody of life can best be seen in our blind veneration of the capitalist free market.

In this blindness, we fail to see that the capitalist free market has no legitimacy whatsoever. The capitalist free market is unjust; it is the instigator of instant or short term economy, thereby damaging any long term economic rationality and prosperity; it is against saving, the pillar of healthy economy; it ignores public order, moral and physical health, unemployment, public services, traffic or air pollution.

The capitalist free market is unjust and unfair because the richer an individual, no matter the origin of his wealth, the more influential he is on the market.

The unfairness and the injustice of the capitalist free market are magnified when it operates in an economy running chronic inflation. This inflation hits the market values of salaries and pensions, much more than the value of the properties, therefore, hurting the majority of the community. What is more, inflation rewards those who contribute to it, those living in debt, while punishing the wisdom of saving and good-house keeping. In fact, chronic inflation suits the capitalist free market as it contributes to the economic instability and uncertainty. The capitalist free market thrives on adventurousness and speculations and these thrive on uncertainty and instability.

The capitalist free market contributes more and more to economic instability, uncertainty and short term economic reasoning and activities because it deals more and more with national currencies, which are increasingly treated as speculative commodities.

Cultivating over-expectation, the capitalist free market creates a great deal of disillusionment and discontent.

The capitalist free market also distorts itself by its insider trading.

Life in a capitalist free market economy is a farcical parody of life mainly because it degrades life's quality. It degrades the quality of life because it prices values. By pricing values, the capitalist free market vulgarises them.

The supreme aspiration of an individual human being is to reduce his fears and anxieties. Being a member of a social species, he can only reduce his fears and anxieties through the community. The community's supreme aim should be, therefore, to create a less unstable, a less uncertain market with which to build a more intelligent long term economy and a better quality of life.

223

With direct and indirect taxation and/or with negative and positive income tax, a community could create a less unstable market. Well timed community's interventions in the fields of supply and demand of goods and services could bring a more lasting market stability.

In contributocracy, people with talents and special humane capabilities would have more chance to come into prominence and join the community's decisions making bodies.

Even a capitalist free market has to be organised by the governments' laws in order to prevent liberalism from becoming libertarianism or libertinism. Unfortunately, democracies and their governments are manipulated by the capitalist economy. The successful people of the capitalist economy have little difficulty in convincing democratic governments that it is in the public interest to organise the capitalist free market in a way which is convenient for the successful businessmen.

Most of the apologists of capitalism and its free market insist on underlining the material achievements of capitalist economy and its market over the past two centuries. These apologists, however, fail to take into consideration the price that we, and future generations, have to pay for these achievements. The price to pay is the ecological crisis, the degradation of life on this planet, global poverty, national and individual debts, crime, violence, brutality, suicides, stress and stress-related diseases and mental disorders. Those who glorify the past walk forward with their heads turned backwards.

Western capitalism is proud of its victory over communism. In its pride, Western capitalism fails to realise that the fall of communism was more due to the failure of an ideology than to Western capitalism's merit. In fact, after a short euphoria, Western capitalism has fallen into a deep depression, a depression mainly caused by the discovery of its own mortality.

Another pathetic comedy is now playing in the former communist countries of Europe.

Like drug pushers trying to induce as many people

as possible to drug-addiction, Western capitalism is trying to convert former communist countries to its economy.

These countries were convinced that as soon as they introduced the privatisation of their economies and the creation of the free market, they would automatically achieve a life style similar to the American soap-operas. What is more, these countries are so naive that they actually believe that the rich West would generously help them to reach the same style of life as those that are successful in the West.

More and more people from these ex-communist countries are now realising that if the West was that generous it would not have been that rich. It is also dawning on them that if the West was so helpful then why don't they start helping their own poor and unemployed.

What is even more tragi-comic, former communist countries are importing the crumbling form of Western capitalism, a moribund ideology, that has been exploited by the most ruthless human element. Many cities of the former communist world are already ruled by the various mafias, organised crime and drug-dealers. Communist corruption has been replaced by a more wide-spread one and with hard foreign currency. What is more, with the free market, the corruption has become openly negotiable.

The corruption, which is increasing with the increase of the cult of individualism and individual freedom, as these increase individual pretentiousness, mainly takes place amongst the public services of these countries, clear evidence that private interest is not in the interest of the public.

Having reduced the importance and the political role of the State and its protection of its citizens from the abuse of individual freedom by the more ruthless, capitalism increases fears and these fears increase an individual's self-interest, selfishness and ruthlessness, which increases corruptibility and corruption. After all, in a market economy, the moral or professional integrity or solidity of those working for a disintegrating State or public interest boils down to a question of price. What is more, with the increase of pretentiousness, there is no government which can merit respect from an individual whose ego is intoxicated by insatiable desires.

Like any other inflation, the inflation of scandals in these countries has even reduced the scandalous effect of the scandals.

I am sure that very soon Western capitalism's conquest of former communist countries will be compensated by an invasion of the invigorating criminal ruthlessness of neo-capitalist mafias.

People of former communist countries are witnessing a significant truth: all ideologies, from extreme private capitalism to extreme State capitalism, have one thing in common: they all go backwards in evolutionary terms, they all prevent us from reaching maturity.

We are not witnessing the end of history but the end of an era of wishful ideologies and beliefs, of pretensions and illusions, an era in which, contrary to natural logic, man played the principal role and woman was just there to help him.

Even man's final refuges of his nationalistic, racial or religious fundamentalisms, so popular at this moment, after their ultimate expansions, will eventually explode. In fact, the major difference between woman and man is that woman's brain is far less seducible by ideological prejudices. The consequences of this is significant. Carrying fears, prejudices reduce us to our reptilian past. Prejudices carry fears because they are usually superior to reality. Leaning less on prejudices, woman's brain operates on a wider and more universal scale than man's, which places her in a better position to deal with our planet's global problems.

Any "post-era" is open to pondering. The post-ideology era will be no different. In this pondering, perhaps, we will realise that Western culture, which has spread throughout the world, is nothing but a mental disorder. Going back over our history of the countless wars and destructions we cannot but conclude that we have been struck down by a dangerous madness, a madness in which man is convinced he is the omnipotent god, a god above nature and its order.

Like his Creator, man is a savage and violent god. Like his Creator, man attributes his negative characteristics to those who oppose or deride him. In fact, these who oppose or deride him are exterminated like wild beasts.

Like his Creator, man creates illusions. Illusions carry excitements and these excitements prevent God and man to realise that in reality illusions are delusions.

In fact, the very idea of an omnipotent God is a mad idea. This wishful God of man's mind, created man in His own image and likeness, therefore as omnipotent as his Creator. This authorises man to try and modify reality and nature in order to adapt them to his own desired image. Would it not have been more fitting with the omnipotence of the Creator if He had created reality and nature to please man, His favourite creation, in the first place ? Man and his God give the impression of immature jokers toying with life on our planet in the most childish and irresponsible way.

Man's pretentious game is drawing to a close. man and his God will either have to mature or to perish in ignominy.

But, one thing is positive: the rest of the living world on planet earth will heave a sigh of relief at the demise of the human species.

227

By the same Author:

"HUMOUR THERAPY in Cancer, Psychosomatic Diseases, Mental Disorders, Crime, Interpersonal and Sexual Relationships."

'Your theories make good sense – and the stories you use to illustrate the theories are delightful."

Norman Cousins who recovered from cancer curing himself with humour therapy.

ISBN 0 9510525 0 0   **Pbk. Price £5.00**

"STRESS ADDICTION". Could it be that we are slowly becoming a species of stress addicts?

Stress seems to help the secretion of our brain's opiates, drugging us often to the point of excitement or euphoria. Perhaps our obsession with individuality and individual freedom, accompanied by depressing loneliness, is nothing but a major source of stress-related brain opiates.

ISBN 0 9510525 3 5   **Pbk. Price £6.00**

Both books are published by:

VITA BOOKS
42 Wandsworth Bridge Road
London SW6 2TH